Help Your Class
TO LEARN

Help Your Class To Learn
Copyright © 1997 Barbara Pheloung

ISBN 978-0-6463309-6-9

All rights reserved. No part of this publication may be reproduced, stored in a retrieval system, transmitted in any form or by any means, electronic, mechanical, photocopying, recording or otherwise, without the prior written permission of the publisher.

Copyright 2020 Jeanette Liljeqvist
jini.lilj@gmail.com

Cover Design - Velvet Creative (velvet.com.au)
Illustrations by Katrina Van Gendt

Note: Robyn Taylor's research report, *Study of Sensory Inegration Combined with Remedial Teaching Methods*, which is reproduced with her permission in this book, remains the copyright of Robyn Taylor.

Help Your Class
TO LEARN

EFFECTIVE PERCEPTUAL MOVEMENT PROGRAMS FOR YOUR CLASSROOM

by Barbara Pheloung

DEDICATION

I dedicate this book to the human spirit that God gave all of us. The wonderfully supporting spirit that He put in my husband, who would have said, if he was alive, "Hadn't you better get busy and write that book." The pioneering spirit in Doman and Delacato. The warmth of spirit in Getman. The generosity of spirit in Sister Yvonne Mary. The honesty of spirit in Judy Tankard. The dedication of Jean Rigby. The humility of spirit in so many of the children I have met. And their desire for life – like the beautiful crocus in my homeland, Canada, that pokes its nose through the frozen ground and snow. It seems to have to try harder but it wants to bloom like all the other flowers. And the spirit of my three grown children – Landy, loyal like his father; Sheila, so buoyant, who flies with broken wings; and 'my baby', Rennie.

Even if I could remember the names of everyone, there is no way I can mention all of the children and friends and authors that have shaped and written this book for me. I thank God that mine is an accepting spirit. I want this book to be the kernel of all the understanding that has been sent my way.

Barbara Pheloung

FOREWORD

Our understanding of the child with Learning Disabilities has taken an enormous leap forward in the last few years. Now our minds are being bombarded with new concepts, described in new language, as we hear talk of genetic predisposition, drug therapy, processing times, brain imaging techniques, quantified EEGs, evoked brain potentials, brain biofeedback, sound therapy and syntonics (light therapy).

With all this new information about how the brain learns, all the flurry of excitement over the rediscovery of processing times, and the swing back to genetic causes of LD/ADD/ADHD, is there any place for such 'old fashioned' motor programs as detailed in Barbara Pheloung and Jill King's last book, *Overcoming Learning Difficulties*? Do they really work? How do they fit into today's understanding of LD? With all the new computer programs being designed to help children hear the short consonant sounds, and with all the new therapies and drugs that speed up processing times, many may ask if perceptual motor programs are still needed for the child with learning disabilities.

This new book gives us the conclusive answers we have all wanted to see and to hear for a long time. In *Help Your Class to Learn* Barbara describes the results of several recent studies in Australian schools where perceptual motor programs have been run. Starting with a study she ran with clinical/educational psychologist, Robyn Taylor, Barbara tells of the exciting work at Oxford Falls Grammar School. Students were tested in all areas before and after a year of perceptual movement work, and the results are exciting, to say the least.

Programs carried out in other schools around Australia are described too. Some of these programs Barbara has been connected with, others not. Everyone whom she knows has done good work in this field has a section devoted to them and their results. Consequently, we are given a wonderful overview of what is currently being done in

Australia in schools. This will be of enormous benefit to any parent, teacher or school interested in this field; the smorgasbord has been laid out for selection.

One of the results to emerge is confirmation of the fact that LD is not just a cognitive deficit. Barbara has released here a study she did on 187 children assessed at her LD centre. They all had significantly high deficits in several of the motor areas. The findings, corroborated by recent research in England by Angela Fawcett, suggest that refined tests of balance might be a very quick way of screening for LD.

This is no news to those who have been working in this field for any length of time. The pioneers, such as Ayres, Bender, Blythe, Delacato, Getman and Tansley, realised how intimately connected were the skills of processing for both fluent movement and fluent academic thinking. I have seen Delacato and Getman at work and what was outstanding about their clinical expertise was their power of astute observation. In their attempt to explain what they saw, they may have used explanations which today could seem incomplete or redundant, but wrong theories do not invalidate accurate observations.

It is therefore left to today's theorists to tell us why, in today's language of 'processing times' and 'brain waves', perceptual movement training is beneficial. How does movement refine and speed up not only proprioceptive (feeling of movement) processing, but also auditory processing, visual processing and the integration of all three to produce balanced, calmer individuals who are more proficient in reading, spelling, maths and writing?

In all the time I have known her, Barbara has been driven by a desire to help as many parents and children as possible, by making available today's knowledge, and telling them how and where they can get further help. There is never any grandstanding in her writings. This, of course, is to be expected of someone whose Christian understanding is of such a depth that she knows we are all part of One Whole, and that there is no point in grandstanding for we are all adding but tiny creative fragments to a very rich mosaic, lovingly designed by God.

Dr Mary Lou Sheil, M.B.B.S(Melb); D.C.H(London)

CONTENTS

CHAPTER 1
Schools could teach nearly all children to read ——— 12

CHAPTER 2
How children develop ——— 21

CHAPTER 3
Nutrition and movement ——— 31

CHAPTER 4
The cost of not helping LD children ——— 41

CHAPTER 5
A perceptual movement program in action ——— 45

CHAPTER 6
A movement program in a small school ——— 62

CHAPTER 7
Movement in a public school classroom in Queensland ——— 66

CHAPTER 8
One concerned mum in country NSW ——— 70

CHAPTER 9
Movement for LDs in a state high school ———— 81

CHAPTER 10
Australian LD resources ———— 87

CHAPTER 11
The conclusion is that this is the beginning ———— 105

Glossary ———— 110

APPENDICES
   1. Assessment at the beach house ———— 114

   2. Teacher checklist for learning difficulties ———— 115

   3. Student record cards ———— 119

   4. Activity cards ———— 120

   5. Articles on learning difficulties ———— 129

   6. Parent interview form ———— 140

   7. Results of word recognition reading test ———— 144

   8. Station sheets ———— 145

References ———— 146

ADDENDUM
Study of sensory integration combined with remedial
teaching methods ———— 148

INTRODUCTION

There is little likelihood that any of our governments in Australia will increase resources to help those with learning difficulties in the foreseeable future. We need to keep pressing for more resources but we can do more than that. We can do a great deal with the resources we already have. These resources are the concerned teachers who are out there, and those parents of the LD children who are keen to help. We also have a few good Australian programs that are well laid out, have been tried and found to be successful. Research has confirmed that LD children have a significantly higher incidence of perceptual motor immaturities.

In 1992 Robyn Taylor, clinical and educational psychologist, and I, cooperated in setting up a perceptual movement program at Oxford Falls Grammar School, Oxford Falls, Sydney. For years, Robyn had had a dream of doing research to prove the effectiveness of including movement and perceptual training in the programs for learning disabled children in schools. She had already started to make her research dream come true by setting up a perceptual movement program at Illawarra Christian School in Wollongong. This program was run by parents and supervised by a teacher with impressive results; the children's increased ability to learn was outstanding. I knew of her great success there and asked her to share her expertise with me at Oxford Falls as she wanted to include more children in her research. She agreed.

I also have had a dream for a long time. Having worked privately with LD children and their families for 20 years, I knew how relatively few children could be reached that way. Not only were we only scratching the surface of those asking for help, but also, there were many LD children who hadn't yet even been identified. There were still many, many children being labelled as lazy, day dreamers, not trying and rebellious, without finding out the reasons for their seeming lack of interest. The developmental problems of these 15 to 20 percent had to be tackled in the schools. These children needed to be identified and helped to gain learning readiness.

I was impressed with how Robyn had done this and I wanted to see it at first hand, so I could write this book to be available for all schools. The Newsletter at my church provided the answer. Oxford Falls Grammar School was advertising for a remedial teacher. Andrew Egan, their wonderful headmaster, gave me the opportunity of a lifetime. Yes, I could set up an approach to learning difficulties, new to that school; we called it The Learning Centre. Without Andrew's special heart for children who have to struggle, and the support and encouragement he gave us, none of this would have been possible.

CHAPTER ONE
Schools could teach nearly all children to read

Many Australians, both adults and school children, are well below an acceptable standard in reading and numeracy. We regularly hear this on television and on talk-back radio. A number of these people have learning difficulties. At least 15 to 20 percent are being prevented from fully using the brains that they have.

It is now common knowledge that there *are* intelligent under-achievers, that there *are* bright children incapable of sitting still or concentrating. We've all heard about the clumsy children and those who don't listen and those who don't observe. We are even beginning to hear children say, "It's not my fault I can't concentrate, it's what my Mum gave me for breakfast". People have become conscious of the effects of chemical sprays and lead poisoning.

But do we really know what to do about it? Has literacy improved? Now that we are aware of all these things, are all children now graduating from school able to read and work out a personal budget? Not at all. It even seems to be getting worse. Reading programs *are not* significantly changing the literacy figures. They help some children quite a bit, but the tide hasn't turned. And yet, within Australia we have the solution.

We have people in this country doing research and finding answers and helping some children. The problem is, that this is happening only in the lives of so few. The lucky ones have parents who can take them to someone who understands enough about LD (learning difficulties) and ADD (Attention Deficit Disorder) to help. Many parents, however, have pointed out to me over the years that it shouldn't be necessary to take children out of school so they can learn.

Everyone in school should have the chance to learn
This book proposes to open the doors for *all* children who are 'behind the eight ball'. Help needs to be offered in schools and it *can be done* because it is already happening in enough schools in Australia to make us sit up and think.

Why so many children still can't read even though the expertise is available
There are many professions needed to help those with learning difficulties but some professionals operate as islands complete unto themselves. Teachers can't be expected to do it all alone because they are not trained as doctors, optometrists, speech therapists, nutritionists, audiologists, psychologists, osteopaths/chiropractors, paediatric physiotherapists or occupational therapists.

LDs need the expertise of all of us and it's criminal for members of any profession to hug their secrets to themselves and think they have 'the answer'. No one has the only answer and the sooner we open the lines of communication between the professions in regard to LD children, the better. 'New boys' keep coming into the field telling everyone they have the answers. I call this criminal because it confuses, misleads and delays parents from finding the solutions pertinent to their particular child. This delay can make the difference between getting the right help or not getting any help at all.

TOO SPECIALISED FOR WORDS
Each like an island unto itself...

Some professionals even denigrate what others do

In actual fact, do any of us know enough about the brain to be absolutely sure that we have all the answers? A number of different people claim that their methods offer the most effective help. Unfortunately, some of us even denigrate what other people do – often without first thoroughly investigating the merits of their work. If you mention the words 'perceptual motor/movement' in some

circles they refer to you as 'old hat'. I was verbally discarded by someone once as the 'hoops and balloons lady'.

In the LD field we cannot afford to keep professional secrets. The child is more important than individual reputations. We need to look to each other to improve our expertise. We need to train as many people as possible, and keep fine tuning that training so that our children will be safe and will be helped.

Identifying the children who are having difficulty

Twenty percent of our school students are at a pre-school level in one or more areas of development. A child aged seven in Year 2 may have the visual skills of a three-year-old. Or, she may be aged ten in Year 5 and still not know which hand she would prefer to write with.

Fifteen to twenty percent of those entering kindergarten haven't yet developed all the skills needed for efficient classroom learning. The problem compounds each year. At kindergarten they may not even be spotted because they are obviously intelligent and don't have to do too much desk work. Each successive year, however, more demands are made on their listening abilities, their eyes, their need to sit still and concentrate and do more than one thing at a time. And when they get to second class or even later, it starts to become obvious that even their intelligence cannot compensate for their lack of maturity.

Why the problem must be dealt with in schools

Schools have to be the place where immature children are given the chance to catch up. Those who are unable to make much sense out of print, out of the black/white board, and have trouble handwriting, all need a variety of visual exercises *daily*. You can be sure that, at present, only a small fraction of students are receiving the good care of vision therapists – those whose parents take them out of school for this and do the exercises at home. The others, however, shouldn't be penalised because they are not receiving help for their eyes. Appropriate exercises can be done *daily* in the classroom.

Children who can't listen, who daydream, and who can't remember enough, can *all* be helped with appropriate auditory perceptual activities *daily* in the classroom. Most of these are not getting any help at all for their problems at the moment. The exceptions are those whose parents take them to a remedial teacher outside school who understands how to stimulate auditory perception at the level of the child's need. We know that a number of classroom teachers will be introducing auditory perception into their teaching but the easiest and most effective way to do this is in combination with movement.

Children who can't write letters and numbers without going in the wrong direction, who can't even get started, let alone finished, with a written expression, who don't know right and left directions, *all* can be helped with daily movement activities in the classroom. Again, few of these children will be having their problems addressed at the moment except for those whose parents take them to movement programs which are aimed at the correct level of immaturity for their particular child. And, of course, those who are now doing daily classroom movement activities.

There *are* schools where teachers are already doing regular perceptual movement programs in their classrooms with amazing results. Much of the rest of this book is taken up with descriptions of what is happening in these schools, who is instrumental in running the programs and what resources are available to help teachers select the best program for their school's needs.

What is the problem with children who are unable to learn easily?

Basically, as I see it, the problem is *in* the brain of children who have learning difficulties – but not because of lack of intelligence. The 'wiring' is loose. Some 'wires' are too short. Information getting in through the eyes to the brain may be incomplete, it may be processed too slowly or it may be confusing. In addition, these children can sometimes hear only part of a sound or part of a word or part of a sentence. To compound the problem, what they *do* hear may be processed slowly and is confusing.

What some children feel through their skin and muscles can also be incomplete and may be processed too slowly or too fast. This becomes particularly confusing when sensations don't match; for instance, when what a child touches, doesn't seem to give quite the same messages as the way he sees it. If the object in question is a pencil he is trying to write with he will experience difficulty. The brain can operate only on what the body sees, hears and feels. Therefore, for those with LD, the brain operates without the correct information that 80 percent of children in the classroom receive.

The two halves of the brain
To make it even more tedious, but all part of the same thing, the two halves of the brains of most of the 'strugglers' aren't cooperating and working smoothly together. The signs of this in those aged seven and over, are that they don't *automatically* know their left from their right sides. It is also likely that they will have difficulty doing more than one thing at a time. Since handwriting and most classroom tasks require the efficient use of areas in both sides of the brain simultaneously, LD children have to struggle and 'try hard' at what may be, for others, quite simple exercises.

Why many classrooms can't help LD children learn
Many children with learning difficulties cannot make sense of what they hear. In the classroom the information to these students isn't always fed in slowly and clearly and with emphasis, *which is what they need*. A classroom teacher who speaks in a soft monotone will *not be heard* by the crippled listeners. Teachers need to speak slowly, with emphasis, and back up their speech with good body language and dramatic gestures, as well as written material and illustrations that will

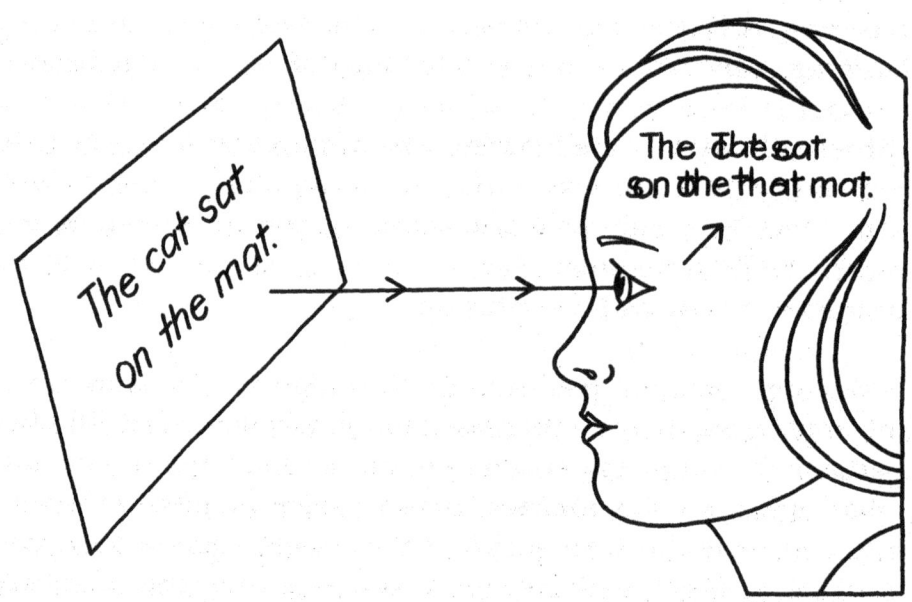

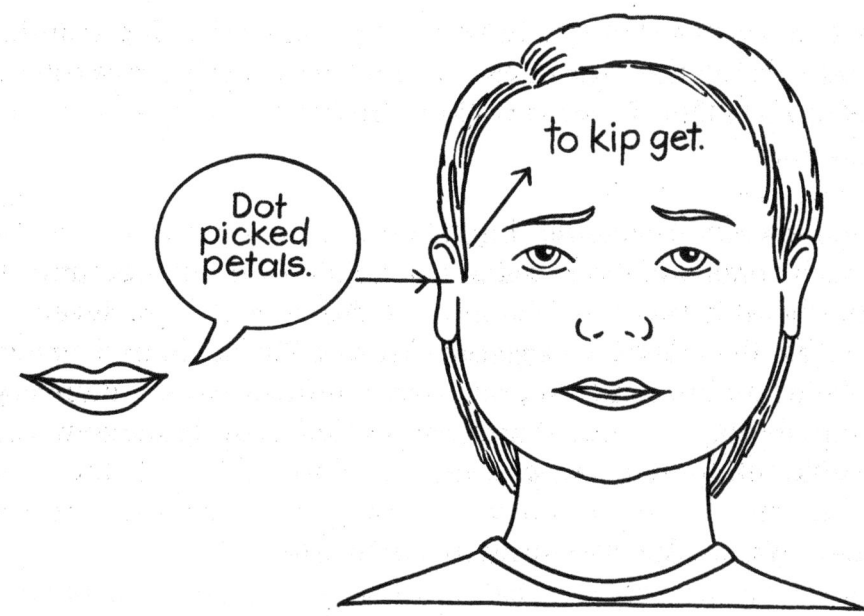

convey and reinforce what they are talking about. When these things don't happen, then much of what is said in a classroom will be totally missed by our poor listeners. After a while, they will give up trying to listen and just tune out and daydream.

They can't remember instructions
Another very real and common disability that our poor listeners can have is not being able to remember a sequence of instructions. This is because they cannot remember more than two or three things at a time, while the rest of the class will have no trouble remembering five or more things. And so, when a teacher, giving a series of instructions, gets to the third or fourth items, the first instruction drops off the register of the child with a poor short term memory. If five instructions are given, our student has no way of remembering the first two or three. "Put your blue composition book away and open your red one to page 29". The implications of this in a classroom are easy to see.

Some cannot use their eyes to learn
Classroom teachers don't always understand that some of their students are poor at observing visually and, therefore, cannot make sense out of a black or white board covered with words. Glare can also erase whole sections of the board for some children. The visual presentation of material also needs to be supplemented by the other ways of getting information to the brain, and through written

handout sheets that don't need to be copied or read quickly. Without this extra help, a whole group of LD children, those with poor visual perception, will literally learn nothing from the board at the front of the classroom.

The majority can't organise anything
A mother's comment about one of these children could easily be, "He wouldn't be able to get to school unless I dressed him". There is the whole area of the ability to organise yourself. The majority of children with LD find organising either themselves or their work very difficult. This is frustrating in a classroom, on a day-to-day basis, and it also makes written expression impossible.

Schools can make this country literate

The very, very good news is that information getting to the brain can be speeded up. This isn't *new* news but various people keep rediscovering this miracle and claiming it as their own. The crux of the news is that immature, confusing and incomplete processing can be speeded up with stimulation. Brain connections can be made more accurate and stable. Most people can learn to listen and to look. The rest of this book is filled with stories of some of those in Australia who are currently helping children to learn more easily and who are willing to help any school do the same thing. Schools can improve the situation by leaps and bounds. They have a unique opportunity to look at *nearly all* children and help them appropriately – because *nearly all* children attend school. Schools can use the right professionals and parents to make this country literate. Parents and professionals alone, cannot, and have not, done this. Nor have schools – *but they can.*

CHAPTER TWO
How children develop

A knowledge of child development gives us the clues as to how we can teach children best. Most of us are far from understanding how our brains work and why some brains seem to be more efficient than others. It isn't necessary, however, that we be brain surgeons but it is necessary that we know about the different stages of child development. The children we are concerned about have missed, or partly missed, some of these stages. They are not mature in their language, or their vision, or their listening abilities or their movement abilities or some of all of these things. In other words, they don't have learning readiness.

For instance, a learning disabled child who is ten years old may be trying to learn in a classroom with the visual abilities of a three-year-old. Or their use of language could be at a six- or seven-year-old level. In the two decades I have been working with LD children of all ages, and with adults, I cannot remember one of them who had the integrated, efficient brain that a child of seven should have. This means that the odds are definitely against them. They *are* behind the eight ball.

It doesn't really matter how they got the way they are
This is an interesting subject for discussion. A number of the parents I've met have suddenly remembered in the middle of their child's assessment that "Uncle Harry was like that". "Actually so was I". There does appear to be a genetic factor. This seems to have been the case in

our family. Maybe because of this genetic factor they didn't crawl or they needed more touching than they got. There may also have been trauma or injury during birth or after. They may have sat in a playpen too much or used one of those 'walkers' or spent their time in child minding centres without enough adult language to model. Maybe they don't eat protein for breakfast. Perhaps they have watched too much television, or did not have trees to climb or roofs to jump off. Yes, it's an interesting discussion but no matter what the reason is for someone's learning difficulty, the solution is the same.

Children with learning difficulties were not ready to go to school in the first place

Readiness is the operative word – *learning readiness*. If we understand what that means, then all we have to do is help them become ready for school learning, whether they are five, ten, twenty or fifty years old. This is why it is so important for us to know about child development. If someone isn't ready to learn academically, why aren't they? What is missing? These missing ingredients are the keys to our understanding. We have to become detectives. What's missing here? What is he trying to cover up? If she can't move her eyes from side to side and focus them she couldn't possibly be expected to read. If he can't write figures in a straight column he shouldn't be tarred and feathered for his poor arithmetic. There is cause and effect. We know the effects so let's look for the causes.

First things first

Again, like a good detective, we have to look into things, searching for causes. We have to understand that God knew what He was doing when He decided to have babies grow up in a certain way instead of dropping them fully made.

And if we are observant, we will have realised that most babies develop in a sequence of stages, most of them the same as one another. It is the ones who don't develop in this normal sequence who can find it more difficult to learn than they should.

The sequence of stages of child development

The following sketchy account of child development may help alert you to this. A few of the goals that should have been reached at approximate ages are listed.

How children develop

By 6 months
A child should be able to roll over which helps break down that imaginary midline wall (see Glossary) which goes vertically down the middle of the body, making coordinated activity impossible. Sitting positions are being explored. They will be learning through the skin, the muscles and the eyes as they reach, grasp and transfer things from hand to hand. They learn a lot through the skin as everything goes in the mouth and as they pat and scratch surfaces. They lay the basis for listening and language through cooing and squealing.

By 12 months
A child should have had plenty of pulling him/herself along the floor as well as many weeks of crawling in a coordinated way on hands and knees. This lays the basis for the two sides of the body to become integrated. Crawling also gives the eyes good focusing practice at the reading distance. It is about the same distance from the eyes to the floor as from the eyes to a book. A year old child should be able to use eyes in a coordinated way, to investigate everything with his/her hands and have learned to release objects. Ears should be giving accurate messages so that language will have progressed to naming special things and a few other words.

By 18 months
The child should be walking quite well and throwing, kicking and chasing balls. Eyes should work well together. There should be a love of blocks, sand and water and much talking to self.

By 2 years
Walking and running well and jumping. Slides and swings should be enjoyable. Visual skills should have improved to the point where things inspected by the eyes are not always touched. Short sentences.

By 3 years
Can climb stairs with alternating feet. Eyes can follow an object *without* head moving as well. Eyes are used more than hands for simple puzzles. Asks and answers simple questions.

By 4 years
Midline wall should have disappeared. Throws ball at target and can catch. Cuts, colours within lines. Talks at length to self.

By 5 years
The majority of children have decided which hand and foot they favour. (Should be on the same side). This might take to seven or even eight years of age to occur and it must be left to the child to decide by experimentation. Should have basic, adequate grammar.

By 7 or 8 years
Child should be fully integrated so that both sides of the body and brain work together efficiently.

Some preschool skills have not been learned, even by adult LDs

Many of those who develop learning difficulties did not crawl correctly, or for long enough and some not at all. This will have made their coordination difficult, focusing of eyes unpractised and exploring of space around them insufficient.

One LD boy I knew, had never put things in his mouth as a baby and he also didn't crawl. This lack of tactile experience meant that he hadn't learned enough about his own body in the best way he had of learning about it – through his skin. Therefore, he couldn't make informed sense out of the space around him because you have to be familiar with your own body's shape, size and ability to move before you will be able to understand about the position, shape and size of things around you. This flows over into two-dimensional things like placing drawings or writing on a piece of paper. Children who can't do this put numbers or words too far over on one side of the paper, or have crooked columns. They find the shapes of geometry difficult to master and when they write figures for number work in columns, they get mixed up as to which number is in what column. The particular boy I referred to had a lot of trouble with number work until he did an amount of basic tactile work, thus laying the basis for understanding space around him.

Many LD people still move their head with their eyes, moving their head from left to right as they read. By age three a child should be able to move the eyes independently of the head. By age four the effects of the midline wall should have disappeared but you will see in the next chapter that 56 percent of 187 children seen at my LD centre still had a strong obvious midline wall.

Poor balance and posture can be detected early by watching a child at play. By 18 months a child should have enough balance to learn to kick a ball. By two years, good balance enables them to walk on tiptoes and jump. Many adult LDs have never achieved good balance and posture and probably find handwriting stressful.

Lack of integration of the two sides of the body is another immaturity common to LDs. The majority of children have decided which hand to draw with by four years. And by seven years they can easily learn to automatically tell their left from their right. Nearly all LDs have to think first, for a second, which is right and which is left. This means that the two sides of the brain are not working efficiently together and that learning will be slower and more stressful.

The Pyramid of Learning

The diagram opposite, the Pyramid of Learning, illustrates children's neurological development in a simple graphic form. Obviously, many of the steps described start to develop earlier and go on together at the same time, but the layout is a way of indicating the order in which maturity should occur. A child's development starts from conception so we need to start to look at it from the beginning. When we see that a stage has been missed or inadequately stimulated then *that is where we start remediation.*

Who and what can help

We start at the bottom of the diagram and look to see what help is needed at each stage. The professionals listed would be able to help the immature areas but, as well, their expertise can provide *guidance for perceptual motor activities*. However, we are not suggesting that parents take their children to all of the listed professionals. For one thing, they are not all available, everywhere. For another thing, a child can be over-assessed. Rather, professionals are available when pieces of the LD jigsaw puzzle don't fall into place. It is helpful too if teachers know which professionals to suggest so that parents can be guided and do not have to run around searching for the right help.

Arousal level/alertness

If a child is having trouble at this very basic level, the arousal level, then he will not be able to concentrate, he will probably be over- or under-active, his memory will probably be affected and he will

How children develop

WHERE ARE THE DIFFICULT AREAS IN EACH LD CHILD?

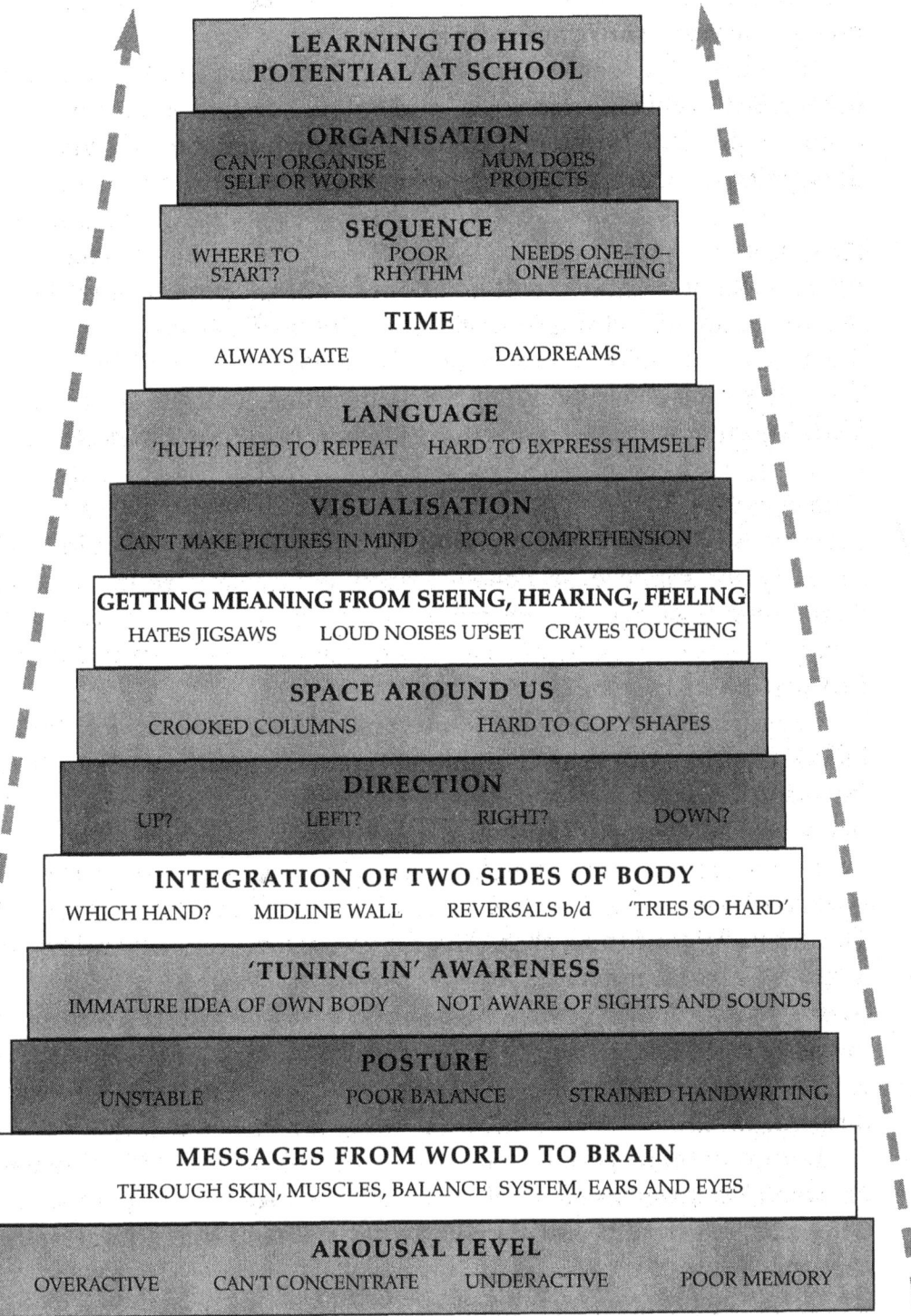

undoubtedly have received the title ADD.
(Paediatrician, naturopath, allergist, osteopath or chiropractor, nutritionist.)

Messages from world to brain
A child must be able to see and hear well and get accurate information through his skin, muscles, joints and balance system.
(Audiologist, developmental optometrist, orthoptist, physiotherapist, occupational therapist, and/or speech therapist.)

Posture
A child who is unstable, will have poor balance, posture and the risk of strained handwriting. Any of the practitioners selected to help with this problem should be experienced in working with children.
(Perceptual movement program, physiotherapist, occupational therapist, Feldenkrais practitioner, and/or Alexander Technique practitioner.)

'Tuning in'
Some children need special help to become aware of their own bodies (size, shape, position), and of the things they see and hear.
(Same help as above, as well as teachers.)

Integration of two sides of body
The symptoms of inadequate integration are poor concentration, inability to do more than one thing at a time, confusion over left and right and reversals.
(Perceptual movement training.)

Directionality
There can be confusion about the directions of left, right, before and after and up and down.
(This should fall into place when a child is automatically aware of his own right and left.)

Space around us
Symptoms of poor spatial awareness are problems in positioning work on paper, writing crooked columns and difficulty at copying shapes. Once we are aware of our own bodies it is easier for us to learn about the space around us.
(Perceptual movement training.)

Getting meaning from hearing, seeing and feeling
This refers to perception – how we interpret what we see, hear and feel. Children who are inadequate in this, dislike jigsaws, get upset with loud noises or don't listen and either hate or crave touching.
(Perceptual movement training.)

Visualisation
Symptoms include difficulty making pictures in the mind, poor comprehension and poor written expression.
(Perceptual movement training, teachers.)

Language
Symptoms are immature use and understanding of language.
(Speech therapists, teachers, and/or perceptual movement training.)

Understanding time
The child who has a poor understanding of time is likely to have poor number work skills and will always be late.
(Perceptual movement training.)

Sequence
Poor sense of rhythm, great difficulty with written expression, can only learn through one-to-one teaching.
(Perceptual movement training.)

Organisation
Symptoms are an inability to organise self or work.
(Perceptual movement training.)

Children are best able to learn if all of these steps are in place by the time they are seven years of age or, at the latest, eight. It becomes obvious that classroom teachers cannot be expected to do more than they are trained for. Teachers can seek the help of other appropriate professionals using this pyramid as a guide for the order of referrals, starting from the bottom. Parents who notice their child has a problem often seek help independently but they can only be expected to follow one thing through at a time. It is likely that if basic things are attended to, then some of the professionals farther up the scale may not even be needed. If professionals cannot be found then a movement program will fill in most of the gaps for most of the children.

Perceptual movement helps so many immaturities

It is obvious just how many areas of difficulty can be addressed through perceptual movement training. If you look, in the next few chapters, at the kinds of perceptual and motor activities that are done in typical school programs, you will see that they match up with the immature symptoms listed in this Pyramid of Learning. This can again be a guide to the correct order for perceptual movement activities.

CHAPTER THREE
Nutrition and movement

Many of us believe that the reason we have got nowhere in solving the literacy problem in the last 20 years is because we have, by and large, missed the two most important things. We have put nutrition in the too-hard basket and we dismissed the importance of movement as 'old hat'.

The importance of providing good nutrition and looking at food allergies

Right at the very bottom of the Pyramid of Learning is the arousal level. The alertness of our children, whether they are too sensitive to everything around them or whether they are apathetic, can depend on several things. Prenatal experiences, inherited tendencies and the child's make-up all play a part. But here I want to discuss the part played by a child's reactions to foods. A child can have an intolerance of, or bad reaction to, certain foods and this can have a disastrous effect on behaviour and learning. Removing the offending food for a period of time often helps. Also, many children have an inadequate diet, handicapping the brain and body from developing to their best.

When I was doing early morning trampolining with some Year 6 boys at Oxford Falls Grammar School I could usually tell what they'd had, or hadn't had, for breakfast. They needed to listen to a series of instructions, such as, "6 jumps kneel, 5 jumps sit-kneel," repeat them and then carry them out. Sometimes, one boy would be quite unable to concentrate and I would ask him what he had had for breakfast.

"Sugar Puffos" or "Nothing". It was a waste of time for him to be there. The brain must have protein and complex carbohydrates, such as whole grains and fruits, especially in the morning.

When we came to Australia over 40 years ago I went to my son's school for my first P and C meeting. I will never forget the looks I got when I questioned their plan to raise money by selling sweets and cakes to the children at morning tea time. I felt like an outcast leper. Has this attitude really changed?

The whole issue of nutrition is a real pain because "everybody else eats junk food" and "I hate vegetables" and "Tom drinks all the milk he wants and he reads okay." It often looks as if there is a conspiracy against parents giving their children good food. A shopkeeper will hand a child a sweet without asking the parents first. Television does everything possible to undermine good eating. School canteens supply meat pies and sausage rolls as if they are going out of style. Even the Sunday School provides the children with cordial and sugar biscuits without checking first with parents. It's really much easier to give in and "at least get some food in them."

If enough of us, however, are determined to give good fuel to our children then this could become the 'smart' thing to do. Some school canteens are becoming leaders in this, or trying to. Could we reward our children with praise and stars rather than lollipops? Could our teachers educate the children in good eating habits? Could we spread correct information about nutrition such as the fact that improved nutrition will improve academic performance? Maureen Hawke, in her pamphlet on nutrition (see References) quotes the New York study published in 1986 called 'The impact of low food additive and sucrose diet on academic performance in 803 New York city public schools.'

The effects of refined sugar

Sugar, on its own, doesn't help anyone to think better. In fact, we don't need any refined sugar at all. It tends to falsely stimulate followed by a low. There is enough natural sugar in a balanced diet.

Some children, however, can actually be put at risk by having too many sweets. They may already have some stresses such as 'poor wiring in the brain' and the additional stress of refined sugar sends them off the planet.

One mother, I know, makes a point of always taking her son late to birthday parties. She doesn't want him to miss out entirely but, in that way, he will have less time to be disruptive as a result of the huge intake of sugar he will get.

Sugar isn't the only offender

There are plenty of statistics to show we are eating too much fat and salt and too much junk food. It is processed within an inch of its life so

that there's not much goodness left to help us think and concentrate. Some people call this food, 'empty kilojoules'. We put on weight with it but we're not getting nourishment for growing and thinking.

Allergies and food intolerance

One of the most interesting figures we got from the analysis of 187 children who came to our centre for help with LD (see Appendix 6), was that 77 percent had marked symptoms of food sensitivity. Some of this intolerance is to perfectly 'good' foods such as wheat, milk and naturally occurring salicylates commonly found in fruits, herbs and spices. It is most unlikely that this sensitivity would be so high across the general population.

There is an excellent book on nutrition and food intolerance listed in the back of this book. There are also dietitions, naturopaths, doctors, allergists and others who can help families with nutrition and food

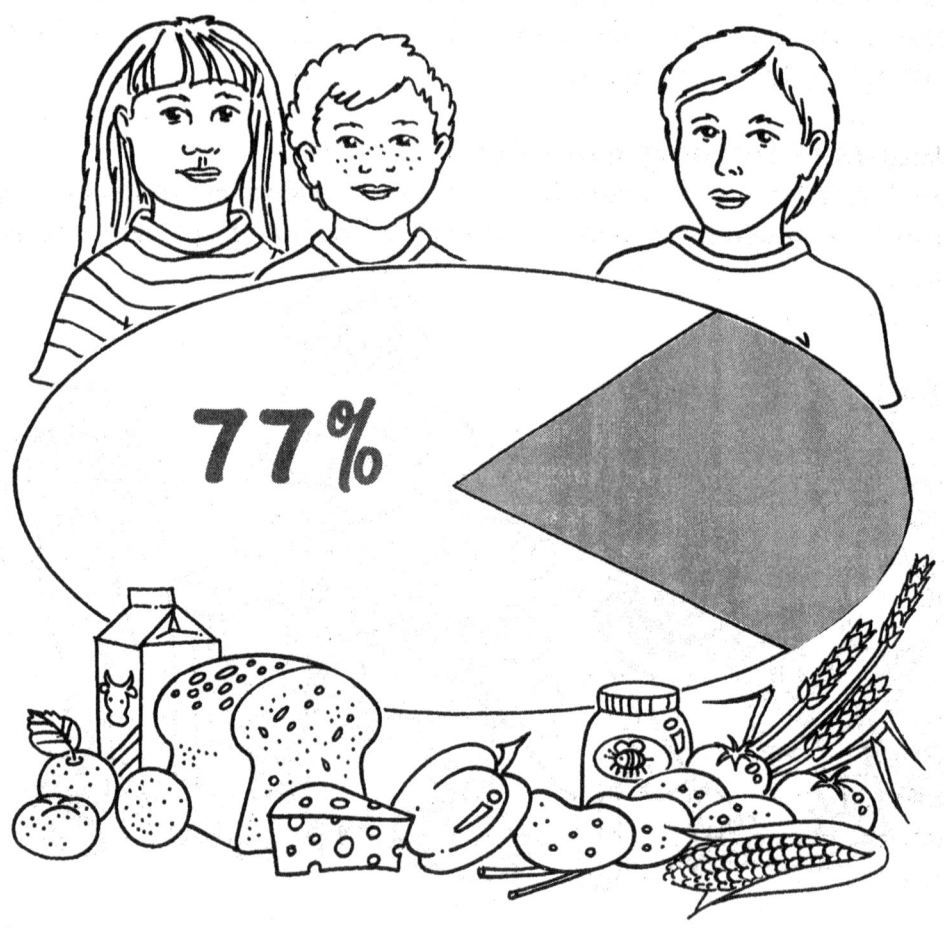

sensitivities. This includes the area of environmental medicine. They have taught us about the effects of lead poisoning on behaviour and the brain – aggression, hyperactivity, lowered IQ. Common chemicals used in our homes or poured into our air and water can affect children who are already over-handicapped.

Glue ear and other disadvantages

Another interesting statistic from the Beach House was the high incidence of ear infections and glue ear. Fifty-one percent of the 187 children tested had had glue ear. There seems little doubt that food intolerance, often a sensitivity to dairy products, makes children prone to ear infections. When there are recurrent infections their cause certainly needs to be investigated so that that particular stressful handicap can be removed.

Handicapping in horse racing is designed to even out everyone's chances of winning. LD children, however, have been handicapped out of the race. For example, an LD child might not be able to use his eyes fluidly and has to move his head back and forth and point with his finger while reading. He could also have a posture and balance problem, so you will see him draped over his desk. He also could have allergies and this could mean poor concentration. His ability to listen has probably been affected by glue ear (see Glossary). These are all stresses. If he has too many of these handicaps he won't even get started in the race, even though, to the untrained eye, he might look like a winner.

The importance of perceptual movement training

I wouldn't want to count the hundreds of times that mothers have told me that they had been everywhere and tried everything but their child was still having difficulties. I would ask them if they had seen a paediatric physiotherapist or occupational therapist and in most cases their reply was, "Oh no, no one suggested that."

The integrating effect of movement has been recognised for a long time. Our special LD children often need more of it, with routines carried out daily, to stimulate them in areas where they lag behind. It is not an overnight wonder cure and it has been discredited in some quarters and become unfashionable in two or three of our states in Australia. Well, that is changing.

Learning through movement and play

Movement is necessary for all growth and change. A baby rolling over to reach a ball gets the brain buzzing between the connections to the eyes, the hand and the parts of the body used for rolling. It is an important step in becoming integrated. It is through crawling that the child receives stimulation of the hands for future handwriting, of the eyes while they look at the floor which is at reading distance and of the coordination of the whole body. These are just a few of the benefits of crawling.

Learning how to climb a tree will help teach a child how to organise himself to meet a challenge. It is this learned ability to organise our bodies which will enable us to get ready in the morning to go to school without Mum nagging at every turn. And it's this same ability to organise that is needed in the classroom. Without lots and lots of walking on walls, bike riding and hop scotch we may fall short in our ability to balance. Balance and stability are two of the most basic foundations for efficient learning because they enable the two halves of the brain to work happily together.

It's the physical activity from play which helps the brain integrate in preparation for academic work. As a child shouts to his friend while chasing him and then, let's say, he trips over a stone, his brain is learning to work as a whole and make sense out of all the messages his eyes and ears and muscles and skin are giving him. And don't let anyone tell you that old story about the bright children who never move a muscle. We don't know how much brighter they would have been if they had got their physical act together!

The same old story

Time and time again, as we worked with LD children over the years, parents kept describing the same physical symptoms. "He reverses his letters and numbers." "She keeps bumping into things." "He's bright and he's got the knowledge but he just can't get it down on paper." "She's off on cloud nine." "He seems to crave swinging and climbing." "He's always touching everything."

When parents came about poor reading, or spelling they also talked about these physical things. Each child was different but the same things kept coming up all the time. We decided at the Beach House, therefore, to put the assessments of a group of our children into the computer to find out the incidence of these characteristic behaviours.

We collated the records of 187 children we saw at the Beach House in the early 1990s. Each of these children had been assessed by a physiotherapist working in the paediatric area and a resource teacher experienced with LD children as well as a variety of appropriate professionals outside the centre. Each of the behaviours that was looked at was graded into one of three categories –

1. No significant problem.
2. Some problems.
3. Significant problems.

The figures in the graphs below only include the children who had *significant problems*. It is obvious that these results would be different from a sample of the general population.

Results of the Beach House study

Seventy-four percent of these children could not organise themselves or their work.
Sixty-eight percent had not established a definite leading side of their body, either left or right.
Fifty-six percent still had an invisible midline wall which prevented the two sides of their body from being integrated. This normally disappears at around three years of age.
Fifty-eight percent couldn't march in a cross-patterned manner.
Seventy percent had an immature vestibular system which meant they had problems with balance and relating to gravity.
Sixty-two percent weren't getting adequate messages to the brain from their joints and muscles. You can be sure that these would be finding handwriting stressful and they would be classified, both in the classroom and the playground, as 'clumsy' ones.
Forty-six percent were getting inadequate messages from the skin to the brain. This would also have made handwriting difficult and be part of the cause of poor body awareness.
Fifty-nine percent had significantly immature body awareness. This would have made awareness of space around them inadequate. They are the ones who couldn't lay out their work properly on a piece of paper or do geometry easily.

LIKELY AREAS OF DIFFICULTY FOR LD CHILDREN

Maturity of the vestibular system	Maturity of proprioceptive system – (messages between brain & muscles/joints)	Maturity of tactile system – (messages between brain & skin)	Maturity of body awareness
At age level 16 — 9%	At age level 33 — 18%	At age level 30 — 16%	No record 9 / At age level 21 — 16%
Some immaturity 40 — 21%	Some immaturity 38 — 20%	Some immaturity 71 — 38%	Some immaturity 46 — 25%
Significant immaturity 131 — 70%	Significant immaturity 116 — 62%	Significant immaturity 86 — 46%	Significant immaturity 111 — 59%

Nutrition and movement

Ability to organise themselves	Leading or dominant side of the body established	Persisting presence of a midline wall	Cross patterning ability
No record 15 — 9%	At age level 10 — 5%	No record 23 — 18%	No record 35 — 22%
At age level 3	Some problems 50 — 27%	At age level 11	At age level 7
Some problems 31 — 17%		Some problems 49 — 26%	Some problems 36 — 20%
Significant problems 138 — 74%	Significant problems 127 — 68%	Significant problems 104 — 56%	Significant problems 109 — 58%

All of the collated symptoms of the Beach House LD children are listed in the Appendix.

Back to the Pyramid

If you look back to the comments after the Pyramid of Learning in Chapter 2, you will see in just how many areas these LD children have gaps. Their basic foundation stones are very wobbly and that is why there is such an unproductive struggle with academic skills. Perceptual movement training which addresses these 'missing links' in each child will bring about the desired learning readiness for academic work.

CHAPTER FOUR
The cost of not helping LD children

We know that there are a disproportionate number of LD people in our jails and in the unemployment queues. This is not merely because they can't read and write as well as others. People who are mentally handicapped also find it hard to read and write but if they are doing it as well as they can, they are perfectly content. LDs know instinctively they could improve and don't know why and there is no contentment. The reaction of some is to strike out in frustration at others, or themselves.

Svea J. Gold, in her book, *When Children Invite Child Abuse* (pp.107-8), refers to a study done by Allan Berman, a clinical psychologist who works with delinquent children in the eastern part of the USA. Svea describes the process he went through in his research and his communication with the courts over these kids. He found that "71 percent of the delinquent kids were on the neurologically impaired list, while only 23 percent of the control group were impaired".

The LD population that I am writing about is not mentally handicapped and many have above average intelligence and so they are acutely aware that they 'should be doing better'. They struggle with failure during all those formative years at school and they adopt behaviours which will prove to themselves and others that they have some special qualities and some worth – the best at getting away with things, the best at causing attention through disruptive behaviour, the best at cutting off and floating away. There have been two young men, relatives of mine, who have taken their own lives in recent years. Both had learning disabilities and found it all too hard.

Svea talks also about a study done on the Isle of Wight in 1976. "What they found was this: the delinquent kids were almost uniformly two grades behind in their reading achievement." (page 109, ibid.)

What LD children have to overcome

Hyperactive children, kids with intolerance to certain chemicals and foods, hypoglycaemic children and Attention Deficit Disorder kids, all have extreme mood swings which cause them to be very high and then very low. This often provokes disapproval from others and this disapproval usually increases the 'bad' behaviour. Unless the proper intervention is given, things get worse and self esteem drops.

Some of these children at risk still have primitive reflexes in their bodies (see Glossary). This means they may occasionally have some involuntary movements which they cannot control. They might experience an abnormal sense of being threatened if, for instance, the moro reflex was still present. This is a primitive reflex which enables a baby to cry loudly for help. After six months this reflex develops into the adult startle reflex. If it hasn't calmed down to a startle reflex there will be a resulting surge of adrenalin which causes anti-social behaviour in much the same way as an allergy to chemicals.

Another LD symptom, which has already been discussed, is the tremendous difficulty they have in organising themselves and their work. It is obvious why they would have trouble in the workplace but they can also have great difficulty in seeing the consequences of their actions. They cannot understand the order or sequence of events so it is hard for them to see how their action now can cause a reaction down the line. When they are reprimanded they don't understand why and they often feel that they are being treated unjustly. This results in a display of the old 'chip on the shoulder' attitude. These things relate directly to drop-out.

Those who cannot accurately perceive spatial relationships will not only be poor at geometry but their skill at ball games will also be affected. If you are not much good at games in the playground you will be made fun of and left out and it is obvious how that can affect your view of yourself and of society. Visual perception, in fact, was found by Allan Bermann, to be "the most frequent disability" (page 108, ibid.) of the delinquent kids.

Ways of coping with disadvantages

My family is fortunate. My daughter has not turned out to be a delinquent, but a brief description of her visual perception problems may add to your understanding of the difficulties that LDs experience. Visual perception and visual memory are a real problem for her. She could never make much sense out of the blackboard. Now, her big problem is remembering people's faces. She's okay if she hears their voice but it is possible for her to have a conversation with someone and then half an hour later or a week later have no visual memory of their face. When she goes to church she smiles at everyone she sees so she won't hurt anyone's feelings. You can imagine, however, what communication problems can arise when you really can't remember what your acquaintances look like.

Those who have not had a good foundation of listening laid in their development will not only be at risk for reading but also in communicating with others. Svea Gold refers to Berman's findings. "A close second was in auditory memory. This was an interesting discovery for Berman, because the reason most people get angry at the learning disabled kids is that they won't do what they are told to do. In other words, it turned out that they were not wilfully disobedient; they forgot almost immediately what they were supposed to do."(ibid. page 108)

The third symptom of most frequent occurrence in Berman's study was a language deficit. It is obvious how poor communication will handicap people getting a job and in the workplace.

The pressure on families

This same immaturity in LD children can drastically affect the home. Because the problem is not understood, a child can develop a complex because his eyes cause him constantly to tip over his glass of drink or because he is clumsy. His mood swings can totally disrupt a home with parents blaming each other. Bedroom chaos, "never listening", a huge sense that he is being treated unjustly and an inability to organise himself can all be extremely irritating. I personally have run into a number of families that have fallen apart under the disruption of LD. Not only have LDs failed repeatedly in front of their peers at school, they haven't done too well at home either.

It is almost sickeningly obvious that we must help these children to be able to learn and as soon as possible. They all need to be helped at school, but even better, before they go to school. There are preschools that are aware of this need. Margaret Sasse's Toddler Kindy Gym is now in many parts of Australia and is highly recommended for any preschool child. Other resources are listed in Chapter 10.

CHAPTER FIVE
A perceptual movement program in action

You can't really write about something unless you have experienced it. I knew that perceptual movement training was the way to go for those with learning difficulties when working with one child at a time. But what was the best way to do it in a school? That needed investigation and practice. I'd like to describe how we did it and what we learned over the three-year period.

Setting up a movement program in a school

At Oxford Falls Grammar school we started from the ground up. No one there was familiar with the importance of perceptual movement training. It was one of the best schools I have ever been in, but neither teacher training nor experience had made them aware of how important it was to have the body of a child ready before learning in a classroom could be optimum. Many other schools are like this. The Oxford Falls staff were, however, very open minded and, being excellent teachers, they wanted the best for their children.

This was scary business. Here was a trusting school with 30 to 40 children whose parents were waiting for them to be helped. There would be others needing help that hadn't yet been identified. There was no room available we could call our own, no equipment and only two-fifths of a teacher to help. (Sandy Egan wanted to learn and she had a beautiful willing heart but no training in the LD field or in this particular approach.) We obviously couldn't help all the students right away. Where should we start?

Which students do we start with?
In the school at that time, one-third of the Year 6 class had difficulties. From Year 5 down to Year 2 there were several students in each class who struggled. In Kindergarten and Year 1 there was an unknown quantity although the teachers were worried about a few. We decided to start with Year 6 because those children would be starting high school the following year. Then, in each new term we introduced another group from each year, starting with Year 5, then 4 etc. as we interviewed parents and increased the number of volunteers we needed. When we got down to Year 1 and Kindergarten, we talked with their teachers about activities for the whole of each class to be done by the classroom teacher.

Preparing the ground
Several things had to be done at once. Staff and parents needed to be prepared for the new activities and approach that perceptual movement training involved. Certain basic equipment was desirable. It was necessary to attract volunteer helpers and make plans for training them. The students needing help had to be identified and then assessed.

Reaching out to the staff
The understanding and backing of the headmaster and of the school board was the essential first step. A number of interviews were necessary to enable a full explanation of the program be given to the headmaster, as well as our gaining a knowledge of the school and what would be an acceptable way to introduce it. Great care was needed to make certain that the introduction of this new method would not go too far ahead of the school's understanding of it.

A meeting of all the teachers was called and this new approach to dealing with learning difficulties was introduced and explained. There was plenty of discussion time over the purpose of movement and the symptoms of those students who might possibly have learning difficulties. This was essential because teachers have generally not been trained in the neurological aspects of child development, nor in the importance of perceptual movement for students whose development has been slow in one or more areas. Teachers were also encouraged to read *Overcoming Learning Difficulties*, or at least parts of it.

A checklist of behaviours typical of LD students in classrooms was also circulated (see Appendix). The teachers were asked to look at any students they were worried about and fill in the questionnaire. If there proved to be a number of 'yes' answers then it was worth thinking about sending them to the movement program. This checklist proved to be very helpful in increasing the teachers' awareness of certain behaviours that they had not identified before as possibly being related to learning difficulties. Informal discussions at recess and lunch time, usually about individual students' progress, increased rapport.

Just as important as the teachers' understanding of what we were trying to do, was the need for us to learn of the constraints of teacher time in a classroom situation. Nothing would work unless it fitted into the smooth working of a classroom.

Communicating with parents

Parents are the best source of information about their own children and their support for the help their child is receiving is essential for optimum results. (This is not to say that teachers don't throw additional light, or even different light, on their students.) We needed the help of parents for two reasons. Firstly, a parent's support is very encouraging for a child. Secondly, we needed parents who could volunteer to help run the program.

A meeting was called near the beginning of the year, which was very well attended, partly because parents wanted to find out what new thing was happening in their school. As well as this, however, the headmaster and several others of us had talked to a number of parents in person and explained the importance of what we were doing with enough brevity to tantalise. Here again the whole approach, purpose and structure of the perceptual movement program was explained, and that night we obtained 15 volunteers and a father who offered to make equipment.

Oxford Falls school has weekly parents' newsletters and we had an article in this every month. It turned out to be an excellent way of reaching parents about various aspects of our program and about learning in general. Examples of these are to be found in the Appendix and can be copied if the source is acknowledged.

Volunteer helpers

Even though parents at Oxford Falls Grammar school are very helpful and caring it was feared that, because a lot of parents work outside the home, we would find it difficult to get enough volunteers. We knew, however, that the enlisting of good volunteers was crucial. We did succeed in finding enough good volunteers to run the program successfully. How?

That first parents' meeting gave us a good start. We knew that not all of those who had put their names down would be able to follow through, nor would they all be suitable. But there were enough to get started that second term with the eleven Year 6 students. We offered to train them in an initial meeting and on the job and this was very encouraging for them. They also knew they would not have to work with their own child.

Another good source of volunteers over the months was from the parents' interviews. Each parent who had a child entering the program had over an hour's interview and in that time they could often gain an understanding and an excitement about the program and then offer to help. Alternatively, they would take home *Help Your Child to Learn* (see References) and after gaining a new understanding of LD from this, they would volunteer at the second interview to help with the movement program. Others volunteered at a later date after they began to see changes in their children. There was more than one grandmother who helped out, as well as several members from the church and friends of friends.

Equipment

We had practically no space to store equipment that first year, so we only asked for a minimum. Our volunteer carpenter made us some balance beams, two scooter boards, some stands to hold rods for leaping over or crawling under, a good collection of bits of timber in different shapes and sizes, and he installed a net for us and a punching bag. We were able to buy two trampolines, a small one for inside and a larger one for outside.

We had the use of several school mats and balls and library books. Some mothers made us beanbags, copied mathematics tables on large cardboard and donated a number of puzzles and two rebounders.

A perceptual movement program in action

A COLLECTION OF USEFUL EQUIPMENT

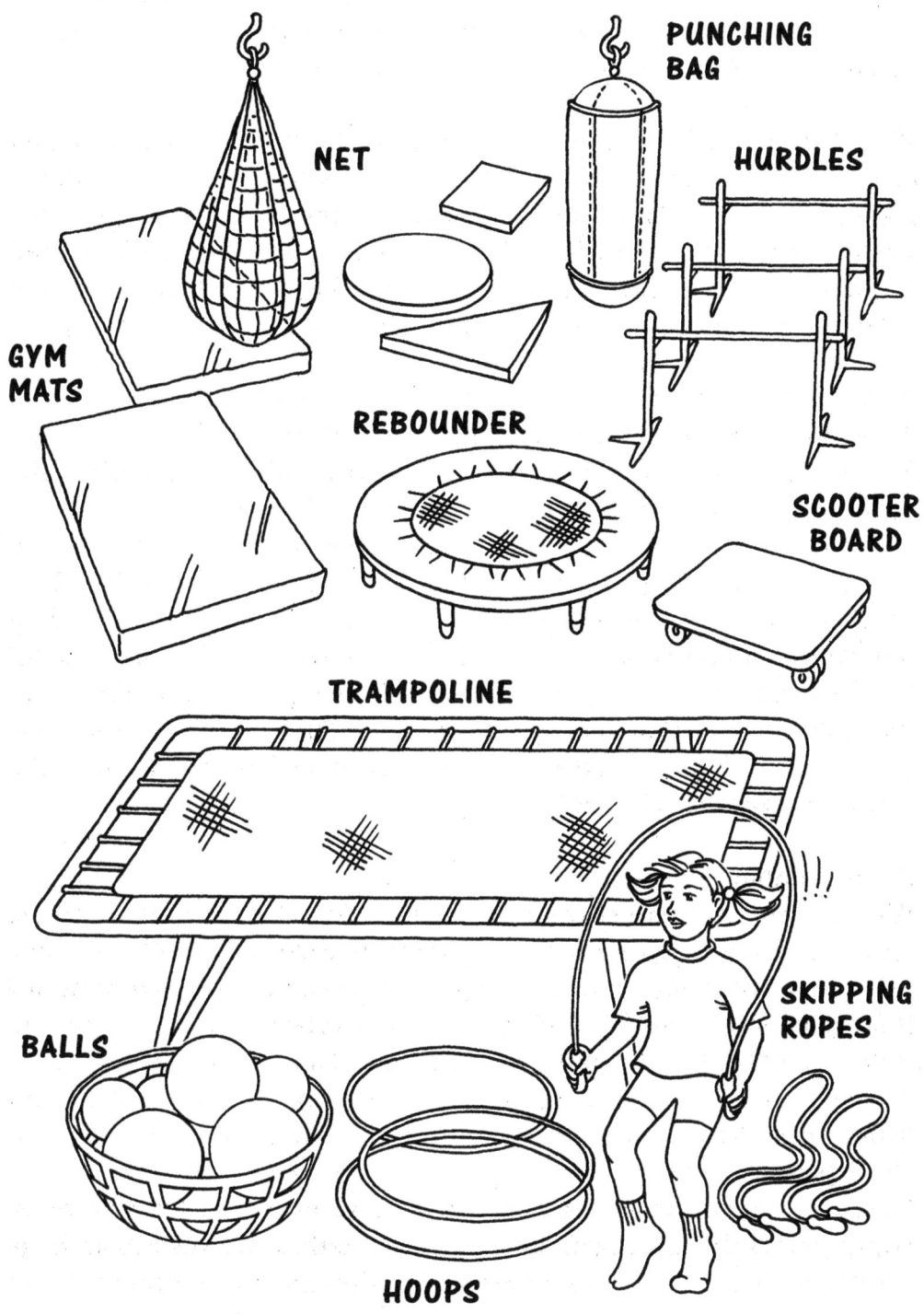

Identification and assessment of students
Students could be referred to the program either through their parents or through their classroom teachers.

Initially there were a number of parents who came in for interviews about their children. Both parents, if possible, were encouraged to come. A history was taken, parents' concerns fully noted and any other help the child had had and the success of that. A parent interview form was drawn up so that as much information as possible could be obtained. Special attention was paid to gaining information about the children's diet, things they craved and didn't like. When the parents answered the questions from *Help Your Child to Learn*, further information was gained about the child. See Appendix 6 for the parent interview form.

At this interview, also, the form that the teacher had filled out regarding classroom symptoms and academic progress, was discussed. Parents appreciated this amount of detail and it was usually easy for all to see whether entrance into the program would be beneficial or not.

An explanation was then given of the purpose of the perceptual movement program, how much withdrawal from the classroom might be involved, possible length of program and what results were expected. If both parents had not read *Help Your Child to Learn*, this was either lent or sold to them because their understanding of the nature of Learning Difficulties was essential.

An additional important part of this interview was in referring the child for any needed assessments that hadn't yet been done. These included such things as doctors or allergists for food intolerance, eye carers, audiologists, paediatric physiotherapists, or occupational therapists and speech pathologists. It was arranged that the mother would send back all reports from any necessary assessments.

When these had all been received, a decision was made in a second short parental interview as to what the next step was. Quite often students needed an assessment by a paediatric physiotherapist or occupational therapist and some of these needed a certain amount of individual therapy. This was then embarked on outside the school for as long as needed. Sometimes a period of time was needed for eye exercises. Often, a child was so over-active or under-active or had such poor concentration that it was best to sort out the possibility of food allergies before doing anything else, or see a paediatrician.

When all these things had been put in place, or at least well under way, then it was time for them to be given a WISC-R, the intelligence test used by the psychologist, Robyn Taylor, with whom I was working. This gave us more information about the student's perceptual abilities and it also served as one way of measuring improvement when re-tested. At the school the students were also each given a Neale reading test, Schonnell spelling test and the Keymath test, all of them age normed.

Structure of the program

People often ask 'What was your program? What did you do?' We actually carried out quite a number of different activities over the three-year period.

For the first year and a half Robyn Taylor wrote the perceptual movement program for each class, on the basis of all the information that she had gathered. The activities had different levels of difficulty and were changed every term. The new activities were based on the children's progress. After about a year, when there were fewer children involved, Robyn's programs were more individualised. She discusses her program and gives examples of it in her research report at the back of the book.

By the time the research project was finished we had two part-time resource teachers for a total of four days. Rosemary Immens had joined the staff with Sandy after the first year. We also had the occasional services of an occupational therapist, Lisa Hughes. They followed the same procedure for assessment and worked out the individual child's needs, putting these on a card. Graded activities were also put on individual cards so that volunteers could look at a child's card and select the activity cards indicated. These activities were found mostly in our book, *Overcoming Learning Difficulties*. There was time in the half hour for each child to do about six activities each session. See the Appendix for examples of students' cards and for activities cards.

Information for volunteers

Information about the purposes of different activities, as described below, was given to volunteers at training meetings, on videos and in meetings with the staff. Those using this book are welcome to give their volunteers this summary, acknowledging the source.

You and they talk! talk! talk!
Talk to the child about everything he or she does.
"Which hand are you using?"
"Which part of your body is starting that roll – shoulders? arm? hip?
"The ball is going up above your head, down towards your feet, to left, to right. Now you tell me which way it is going as I move this ball above you while you are lying on the floor."
"We'll count together as you hop."
"You are so good at counting, can you say the alphabet while you punch the bag?"
"Tell me everything you are doing as you do it."

Right and left
Ninety-nine percent of the children will have some confusion over their own right and left sides. They won't automatically know their left from their right. They may also be unsure of which is their dominant side. They may use their right hand for some things and left for others. Or, they may be right-eyed and left-handed and be unsure of which leg is their leading one. We want them to be dominant on one side of their body if possible, or at least have the eye and the hand the same. Just be conscious of this and let the teacher know of any changes.

Vestibular activities
The majority of students who have learning difficulties will be immature when it comes to exercises that help the body adjust to gravity. Some will be nervous about swinging, spinning or climbing. Others will crave these activities. Both of these groups need vestibular activities as part of their movement program but you must watch that you don't give them more than they want. If they feel sick at the stomach, they have had too much. To counteract this, have them jump, with two feet, hard, up and down on the floor. Vestibular activities include the trampoline, mini-tramp, rocking, rolling, scooter board, swinging and climbing.

Flip flops, crawling and creeping

These are explained in detail in the Appendix and are useful for all LD children. Many will not have done enough as babies and some will have missed this stage of development altogether. It provides the basis for good vision, handwriting, balance and integration of the two sides of the brain. Do this as the first activity as they may find it tedious, then do an activity they like. When they are able to talk and move at the same time get them to talk while doing it. They can count, they can listen to the ticking clock or a metronome and count and crawl in time to that, they can say which side they are moving when doing unilateral flip flops, crawl or creep, count backwards, say the alphabet.

Handwriting problems

When a child finds handwriting stressful the first things to do are the crawling sequence, punching bag, hanging and moving on overhead bars. Later on, many fine motor activities can be practised. Some of these are found in *Overcoming Learning Difficulties*. Below is an example of poor posture while handwriting.

Sequencing

Many children can't remember, or do, very many activities one after the other without forgetting. If a child has sequencing immaturity there should be a note at the top of his card to record how many instructions you can give him and expect him to remember. As he becomes confident, increase the number and note it on the card.

Tactile stimulation

Some may crave skin touching, others may dislike it. If their card says they dislike it be careful to touch them only if they agree to it. Both groups need rolling (good on different surfaces), the crawling sequence, pillows and blankets to cuddle in.

Eye movement

This can be done while doing the other activities. Encourage them to watch their hand as it hits the punching bag. Different coloured spots could be put on the bag. Eyes are needed to keep their body straight as they are rolling.

In the crawling sequence they must be reminded, if necessary, to keep their eyes on the forward thumb. Watching the moving ball while lying on the floor is excellent. Practising looking alternately at something close, then something far away, will help their white/blackboard copying.

Learning about time

Those who are poor in mathematics will be immature in understanding time. Go slowly and don't increase the time until they are proficient with the level they are on. Get them to listen to the ticking of seconds on a clock and then do punching, crawling, hopping in the same rhythm of the clock.

Have them do a variety of activities for 10 seconds, then 20 etc. as they watch the clock. Then, do similar activities for similar lengths of time without watching the clock. Do some activities for one minute while you time them. Similarly for three minutes with an egg timer.

Basic bounce

This is the trampoline bounce in *Overcoming Learning Difficulties* in which you will need instruction from the staff.

Recording the child's progress
This can be done simply with a half tick (/), a full tick(✓) and a crossed tick (✗).
  / = Has attempted it and found it hard.
  ✓ = Can do it but not very well.
  ✗ = Proficient and easy.

The time involved for each child

Children were withdrawn from class for half an hour three times a week, preferably Monday, Wednesday and Friday – the occasions spread apart as far as possible. Volunteers worked with one child at a time. There were four to six people in the room at once, depending on the size of the room. Outdoor areas were used whenever practical. Each child's progress was recorded and this was sent to Robyn at the end of each term. When the teachers themselves started writing the program this was done at the end of each term or in school holidays.

The average length of time spent in the program was one year. For each child it depended on three things.

  A. Improvement in ability to do the program.
  B. Reported improvement by the teacher in the classroom.
  C. Reported improvement at home in attitude and application etc.

At the end of the program each graduate was re-tested with all the tests they had been given initially. The results, in detail, are in Robyn Taylor's research. They can be summarised as follows:

A. Improvement in concentration, getting it together, confidence and reduced frustration was reported from both parents and classrooms.
B. Perceptual abilities improved dramatically so that children could begin to feed their brains correct information. Note improvements in WISC scores in Robyn's research.
C. Academic work improved. (See results in research.)
D. When traditional remedial work was given to graduates from the program they improved quickly in a normal way rather than struggling with little result as they had done before.
E. Improvement in academic work and confidence continued to improve after the movement program had ended because the groundwork for learning had been laid.

What did we learn in the first two years?

One thing we learned was that systems needed to be simple. Activities were put on cards which were applicable for any student but graded in difficulty (see Appendix 4). After assessment the correct activities card was selected and the child progressed through it at his own rate.

The importance of feedback

To receive feedback from the volunteers the organiser of the program had a short talk about each child with the volunteer involved every two weeks. This only needed to be for a couple of minutes and was done in an informal way. In asking about a child's progress she would quickly find out if a child was improving, happy or finding it difficult. If the child was being uncooperative the program was probably too hard or too easy and needed adjusting. This also told volunteers that their work and opinions were very valuable.

Gathering feedback from classroom teachers was always difficult because teachers are so busy and many of them at first were looking for instant results. A climate of understanding needs to be built. A few minutes grabbed at lunch time, on the playground or at recess will get the necessary feedback from teachers and also reassure them. They need to know that academic results won't be instant but there will be other improvements first.

"Has concentration improved?"
"Is he better at sitting still?"
"Is there less daydreaming?"

Relationship between classroom teachers and those that run the movement program can also be strengthened by giving teachers photocopies of the reports and questionnaires of any of their students. The information that is discovered about these students is very valuable for the classroom teacher to have.

Collecting feedback from parents was always difficult. They often didn't know what changes to expect but when questioned they came forth with a number of improved attitudes and behaviours. It is felt that forms asking parents for feedback should be sent home on a regular basis. This would also help to keep the parents more in touch with what was going on at school.

The need to explain the program
It is essential to continually keep educating both parents and teachers about the rationale and purpose of the program. There are always new teachers and new parents who haven't heard about perceptual movement training. There can also be a constant barrage from the old guard who say:

"To learn to read, keep looking at a book", and
"To improve handwriting, do more".

There are many people who don't understand that to prepare a child *before* reading and handwriting are attempted will ultimately save time, will have more successful results and is certainly less frustrating for everyone. Parents and teachers need reminders about the length of time needed to become ready to learn – normally about six months to a year. They need to realise that the ideal would be to combine remedial work with movement but that because we have to use volunteers to get anything done at all we can't expect them to act as trained teachers as well. If everyone is patient they will see that once the perceptual movement base is laid, something volunteers can do, then the remedial teaching that follows will be easy and much quicker because of the movement program.

Assessment by a professional
All entries into the perceptual movement program at a school need to be referred first to a paediatric physiotherapist or occupational therapist for assessment. Our school found that it worked well to refer all children to the same therapist who became familiar with the program's need for information in order to plan well. She would often make suggestions as to suitable activities. This particular therapist also came to the school occasionally to check on the children's progress so there was excellent follow-through. We started off the first year thinking this assessment was *desirable*. By the end of the third year we knew it was *essential*.

Who does the assessment of the assessments? At Oxford Falls school we did it as a group – Robyn Taylor, Rosemary Immens, Sandy Egan and myself. It will vary from school to school depending on who is available. If there is no one with experience in the field of perceptual movement then follow one of the set programs described in Chapter 10.

Limits of a movement program

A school movement program is not equipped to help severely affected children. This is only a small percentage of children, probably one or two percent. Their needs are beyond the experience of volunteers and teachers and when these children don't receive prior suitable therapy they end up staying in the movement program far too long, with limited results.

The parent interview will guide the parents as to the correct professionals to go to. The physiotherapist or occupational therapist will be able to give further guidance. When this treatment is completed the school can be guided as to whether the movement program will then be of benefit or not.

There will always be a question as to whether we started at the right place or not. Careful thought has to be given as to whether you start first with the youngest and include the older needy ones as you are able, or do as we did, and start with the older ones.

Perceptual movement for the Infants Department

The other thrust at the whole child approach that was introduced into Oxford Falls Grammar School was into the Infants department. We had made the decision originally to start with Year 6. This decision was acceptable at first but as time went on and we were into the last term of the first year, the Infants Coordinator, Bronte Waller, became concerned that, so far, we had only got down to including Years 6, 5 and 4. "When were the Kinders going to have a go?" By this time, Bronte often relates, her whole approach to teaching had been turned around and she didn't want her children to miss out. Neither she nor her staff had ever been presented before with the neurological development of children, or the total child approach. Oxford Falls had an exemplary Infants Department and yet they knew very little about the importance of nutrition, basic learning readiness or the part played by other professionals.

During our second year at Oxford Falls, Bronte became more and more concerned for her 'babies'. As she learned about the immaturity we were finding in the older children, she knew that this was present in a number of her children. They needed a chance to get fixed up before they left the Infants Department.

It became obvious that the perceptual movement program should be done with all the children of the Infants Department. This had probably become obvious to Bronte long before that. She courageously took on the job of detailing a program, consisting of five activity stations, from books I had suggested to her. These included simple hoop activities, working up to skipping with hoops; throwing and catching bean bags; throwing, catching and bouncing balls; progressive activities with ropes; and obstacle courses which involved crawling, scooter boards and a balance strip. At the end of 1994, she and I gave a simple perceptual motor test to all the prospective Kindergarten children who had registered for 1995, the third year we were at Oxford Falls. The test we used that year was the South Australian Motor Coordination test referred to in Chapter 10.

During that year, the Kindergarten teachers each took their class outside under the lunch time shelter, for three half-hour periods a week. At first, they planned to change or extend the activities each week. Year 1 classes were soon included and they did exactly the same basic program which included crawling, rolling, throwing and catching skills, balance, left/right, hopping, skipping, body awareness and the integration of the two sides of the body.

As the year progressed, however, the weight of the Infants Coordinator's responsibilities of being head of a very fast-growing Infants department, as well as a classroom teacher, meant that fewer and fewer changes were made to the movement activities. At the end of the year, the teachers met with me to review what had happened during their first year. They felt guilty that during the latter part of the year, they had basically been doing the same activities for a whole term. But the children had not let the teachers stop. Those children who were good at the activities, just enjoyed doing them and achieving. The children who found it difficult at the beginning got to be as capable as others through the constant repetition.

The children loved the structure and they were able to set up the equipment themselves. They went around the stations in their classroom grouping, so they knew exactly whom they were to be with. The teacher spent most of her time at the throwing and catching station. Parent volunteer helpers had been decided against but the teachers felt that the children responded positively to this. Each group had its own leader and this sense of independence seemed to be interpreted to mean, by the children, that they were responsible for their own learning. The teachers, as well, had an enjoyable time because their children were so eager to get outside for 'gym'.

And there was an added bonus. The small number of children who obviously weren't improving, came to be easily identified by the teachers. These were referred on, through the parents, for additional outside help from the occupational therapist. Lisa had become involved with helping the older LD children. She also started to come down and observe on occasions and then make recommendations as to which children in Kindergarten and Year 1 needed additional help.

So these were the positive results of Bronte's coming to understand the 'total child approach'. During the next year, however, the year of writing this book, 1996, they ran into a few hitches which slowed them up. The Infants Department grew so fast that there are now full enrolments until the turn of the century. The Infants Coordinator's responsibilities have been extended even further and it has become obvious that more understanding of the whole child approach is needed by some of the other teachers in the Infants Department. They are all young, some just out of college, and none of them were trained at college in the neurological development of human beings, the way God planned we should develop.

Bronte is more convinced than ever, that her 'babies' need to be ready to learn academically before they leave her department. She is now able to reach parents with confidence when they first approach her to enrol their children. She refers a number of very active poor concentrators to paediatricians, to allergists and to the occupational therapist. She talks to the parents about good nutrition. Their ears and eyes are all checked before starting school and some of them go on to therapy with behavioural optometrists. If listening is a problem, the teachers are made aware of this. A few children were asked to wait a year. Bronte has stated that in this year, 1996, all the children in Kindergarten who are at risk, were identified by the end of first term.

Her dreams of continuing an even more effective movement program may need to wait on a seminar or workshop or some sort of hands-on training program for her teachers, conducted by suitable specialists. In the meantime, the Kindergarten and Year 1 children like it just the way it is. Year 2 children who have been through the movement program may want to go on to sports. Year 2 teachers are traditionally expected to prepare their children for sport. What better way to do this than to involve the occupational therapist and special education teachers, asking them to point out what developmental building blocks are missing in any of the children? If T ball is the aim, then 'pre T ball training' can catch the children's imagination and improve their academic work at the same time.

CHAPTER SIX
A movement program in a small school

The Head teacher of Berowra Christian Community School, Alan Reynolds, heard about our movement program at Oxford Falls through a friend. He had been concerned about the direction to take in helping those with LD in his school. The use of perceptual movement training was new to him but he wasn't going to close his mind to anything that might help, without trying it.

Alan came over to Oxford Falls with two parents who were also teachers, Felicity Webb and Diane Willams. They were willing to volunteer their help with LD children at the school. They had only four hours of observation and discussion with me and then they went home, armed with some things to read, books to buy (see References) and a possible movement program to purchase (see Chapter 10). It seemed a lot to digest at once; I thought I'd better give them lunch to make them feel that their trip had been worthwhile.

True to their commitment to children, when I was next in touch with their school at Berowra, I found to my delight that they had purchased the Movement for Learning video and manual (see Chapter 10) and they had put the program into practice that year.

They had targeted the children at risk from Years 1 to 6 as well as their whole Kindergarten class of 15 children. When I went over to visit them at the end of the year it was exciting to hear them talk of their progress and experiences.

Making a start

They did the Movement for Learning program for half an hour twice a week with each group during 1995. They had a few other parent volunteers who were particularly helpful. The older group went first and they assisted in setting out the equipment for three stations of activities. With the LD students each of the three groups had a leader, the three oldest boys in the program. Whenever parent volunteers were not able to come these student leaders filled in. As well, when necessary, they helped out with the Kindergarten program. In some ways these older boys were the real stars of the program.

All of the children "were very, very keen". The movement program was one of the highlights of the week for the Kindergarten children. It was well structured and they knew where they had to be and when. At the beginning of every session, Felicity conducted stretching exercises which she considered an important preparation and then the suggested warm-ups. There was rocking and the crawling sequence of flip flops, first unilateral and then cross-pattern. There were several new activities each week and the leaders emphasised the importance of listening carefully. After the activities were explained, the children were expected to repeat back what they were about to do. Then a discussion followed with the children, of what was first, second and third. They loved it. At the Open Day at the school they had the parents doing the cross-pattern static swimming (flip flops) with "the kindies laughing at them." The volunteer Mums were also "very, very keen". One of the Mums impressed everyone, one Monday, when she did the star jumps while she said the alphabet backwards. Even though the program was conducted for only half an hour a week, Felicity, Alan and the helpers saw a particular improvement in the gross motor skills of the Kindergarten children.

There was another benefit from the Kindergarten movement program which occurred when they were given their perceptual motor assessment by Felicity and their teacher in the third week of February. It identified a couple of children they felt needed extra help. One boy was referred through his parents to an occupational therapist and one went to a behavioural optometrist and found out he was colour blind.

Felicity also pointed out that there was a relationship between those who were disorganised in the classroom and those who needed the

Help Your Class to Learn

most help with movement. The ones placed along the front of the movement class, because they needed maximum assistance, turned out to be the ones having most difficulty in the classroom.

The older LD students had improved physically as well, some more than others. There had also been some noticeable academic improvements. Peter's comprehension had improved eighteen months during six months of the program with no other change in his remedial program. The only addition had been the movement program which he loved. John improved in maths in six months from the forty-fifth to the seventy-fifth percentile. He was also receiving sound therapy at that time.

But there were questions
The questions that Alan and Felicity posed to me were these. "We don't know if our LD children have had enough of the movement

program or not. There are still problems with stressful handwriting and confusion with left and right. Do we continue? If so, what do we do?" "We know that our Kindergarten children loved the program and improved a great deal in their gross motor skills, but would they have done the same anyway, just from skipping, running and throwing balls in the playground, as well as becoming a year older?" "It's hard to get around to the thought that movement can actually change academic success."

What have we learned?
In a nutshell – willing parents or teachers can 'have a go' and conduct the program successfully in a school situation, even without a full understanding of the theoretical basis. However, it was also seen as important that the staff have a fuller understanding of the total child approach and the place of perceptual movement training if this approach was going to continue. Four hours hadn't really given this Head teacher and his two parent volunteers a fair start. What we are talking about is changing teachers' perceptions and the way they look at children. This may need one or two teacher training seminars because very little of this understanding of neurological development has been taught in Teachers' Colleges (see Chapter 10).

At Berowra Christian Community School the movement program had been carried out by two keen and competent mothers who volunteered to work under staff direction. The second year, a teacher on the staff participated. This teacher, the Kindergarten teacher, already, after six months, has started to catch the understanding and excitement by helping Felicity. It is essential that this understanding be gained by others in the school or else when those volunteers and staff leave, so will the movement program.

CHAPTER SEVEN
Movement in a public school classroom in Queensland

Judith Hallin first attended an ANSUA training course (see Chapter 10) in Queensland in 1978. The total child approach and helping children become ready to learn, made great sense to her as an experienced teacher. She was working at that time as a resource teacher in a private Catholic school. For the next 13 years she included the ANSUA movement activities with her remedial work.

Working with remedial students
The way Judith arranged her schedule was to arrive at school each morning at 7.30 a.m. to do the program with her remedial students before school started. Parents were asked to agree to have their children at school early four days a week; it was a condition of their being in her remedial program. They were also asked to commit themselves to this for a year. Judith had a 99 percent success rate with attendance. She had made it quite plain that remedial work without the ANSUA program would be a waste of time. She also asked parents at the initial interview if they were willing to participate on a certain day each week and to regard that commitment as of vital importance. This was 90 percent successful.

Judith did the basic ANSUA program each year – flip flops, slides, creeping and cross-pattern walking. She also used the monkey bars. She ran the program in the library. The early comers moved back the tables, then did scooter board and as a reward got an early mark. The others put the tables back.

As parents heard of her success they would come independently and ask if their child could attend. She also did extension work with bright children who obviously lacked some skills to achieve as well as they should. If they wanted her to help them, the condition was that they attend the ANSUA program as well.

A movement program for the whole class

With the amalgamation of schools (the private school became part of Catholic Education), Judith was given a Year 4 class and could no longer work solely with her precious special children. She relates that she played it pretty quiet at first, taking her class down to the monkey bars and doing balancing activities in the classroom. Then, later, she booked the bingo hall for two mornings a week from 8.40 a.m. to 9.30 a.m. and on Fridays from 1.45 p.m. till 3.00 p.m. "We're managing to do the exercises on a bit of cork at the end of the bingo hall. We do the slides and the creep there and then do a full roll to one end of the hall. Then we do our flip flops, half rolls and then three lots can go down together on the cork floor doing the creep or the crawl."

When I was talking to Judith about this, she had only been doing this more intense program for three weeks. During first term, and the first part of second term, she had had a low movement profile. She was amazed, however, at the results even then. That last two weeks of term had seen the preparations for Book Week. The children were doing their written expression, going through the first draft, then the second and next, the conference. All 34 children had got up to publication level by the end of term. Judith and her parent helpers noticed how painless this had been. Judith had trained a few parents to help her conference with the children and they wondered if they were really needed after all.

"The ability to organise their thoughts had been helped as well as the ease of getting it down – both handwriting and written expression. That is actually tremendous because I thought I could never get 34 children up to publication standard as I'm a bit of a perfectionist. I won't have garbage."

On September 8, of this year, 1996, Judith wrote me a letter to send some handwriting samples which I had asked for. Those, below, are from two of her students ,'before' and 'after' the movement program.

Help Your Class to Learn

Child 1
First sample on March 8 and second one on September 4, 1996.

Child 2
First sample typical of work produced on July 12, 1996. Second sample was done on September 4.

When Judith sent these handwriting samples she also told me of how she was extending the program. She is working with the other Year 4 teacher, with their combined classes numbering 68 children, for four mornings a week; and on Friday afternoons "we do a fitness program, line dancing and relaxation exercises."

Originally, when Judith was exercising her own class, two mornings a week, she was also doing the same for the other Year 4 class on two other mornings. The other teacher took the free class for the Sports Carnival practices. When 'the carnival was over' they started working together with all 68. "In the last two weeks we have 'cross-patterned' the children. They come into the hall (each class has a separate place to put shoes and socks) and as far as possible a designated place to lie for flip flops (wearing old T-shirts over uniforms). We have put them into partners, so that one watches and assists the other doing the flip-flops, then, the roles are reversed. We then line them up, five to a line, and they do the cross-pattern slide down the cork. I start them off, then my teaching partner watches them from about halfway. They line up in the same rows at the other end, and when everyone is finished the slides, they do the cross-pattern walk back the other way. (Illustrations for these are in Appendix 4.)

"One class then gets shoes and socks on and the other teacher takes them down to the playground to go across the overhead ladder. While he is there, I do cross-pattern crawl, full rolls, tyre, exercises on the mini-trampoline and, maybe, a relaxation exercise. Next day the classes rotate in these activities."

Judith also sent the results of six children using the St Lucia Word Recognition Test, first done on 12 July and redone 30 August – 7 weeks apart (see Appendix 7). The average improvement for these children over the seven weeks was 7.7 months. This is an amazing result when you consider that one child didn't improve at all because he played up too much during the exercises.

CHAPTER EIGHT
One concerned mum in country NSW

Gerardine Hill, who lives near Griffith NSW, is a remarkable Mum. She has a daughter with learning difficulties and when she realised what the difficulty was she moved mountains to find answers. Their telephone bill reached new heights because of STD calls to universities, SPELD, LD support groups. She bought books on the subject and she read them. She gathered around herself a group of friends and other mothers who were similarly concerned about their children who were struggling to learn. The Griffith Learning Support Group was formed in November, 1992.

One of the books that Gerardine read was *Help Your Child to Learn*, my first effort. She suggested to the Support Group secretary at that time, Karen Krieg, that she phone and ask me to go to Griffith and give a talk on LD to parents and teachers. She was concerned that there was nothing in Griffith to help the school strugglers there.

This remarkable lady organised a large group of parents and teachers and we had a wonderful day together. I have been impressed over the years with the rural communities where I have spoken. There is such a sense of community support for each other and a dedicated concern for those in need. Griffith was no exception.

In my talk I explained the nature of learning difficulties and the total child approach. My message was twofold. First, the needed professional resources that can be found in Sydney can also be found in the country. Hospitals and health centres had audiology departments as well as physiotherapists, occupational therapists, and sometimes speech therapists. These might also be living in small country towns, bringing up their families and willing to help at least part-time with LD students.

Most communities had access to paediatricians and naturopaths. There should be a knowledgeable osteopath or chiropractor within 100 kilometres. There are behavioural optometrists within reach. Feldenkrais practitioners (see Glossary) are spreading throughout Australia as are educational kinesiologists. Toddler Kindy Gymbaroos are springing up in many communities and they will usually respond willingly to encouragement to run a program for older LDs. It is basically much the same as they run for their preschoolers. Country people might have to travel to a near-by town to find everything they need but the important key is knowing the professionals who take into account the total child. Those who think they have all the answers are misleading.

The second thrust of my message was that a simple movement program done in schools can go a long way towards laying the foundations for learning that were missed before school. And I believe that there are teachers everywhere who would respond to the logic of this approach.

The Infants Assistant Principal of Griffith East

One of the teachers who came to the seminar that day was Norma Marin, the Infants Assistant Principal of Griffith East Public school. The necessity of learning readiness made good sense to her and she also started reading some of the suggested books. Within a few months, after discussions with her Principal, she was on the phone to me to arrange a day's seminar more specifically targeted at teachers. As good as her word, early in 1994, Norma gathered up 60 teachers from Griffith and surrounding towns and country areas to learn more about how to help their puzzling LD students.

This proved to be an exciting day. Country towns take these things seriously and there was the usual television, radio and newspaper coverage. Out of this seminar, a number of teachers were encouraged to start movement programs, in their own schools.

In July 1996 I went back to Griffith. In the 1994 seminar I had suggested that teachers could get further training in this approach from Judy Bulluss and Peter Coles from Victoria (see Chapter 10). Wonderfully, they had already arranged for three of their courses and I was going to be able to sit in on their third one and talk to a number of the teachers I had already met.

Starting the ball rolling

I had heard bits and pieces about what was happening at Griffith East school so I was anxious to talk to Norma. She had started right after my Griffith workshop because she had been looking for something like this for a long time. "I've seen so many teachers working hard, really working hard and putting in a lot of time and the children would improve. But then if you have a holiday or something, they forget, and then you're going backwards".

In 1984 Norma had gone to an Educational Kinesiology seminar in Griffith which started giving her some answers. She became hungry for more information. Our seminar which followed in 1994 seemed to "fill in the missing pieces of the jigsaw". There was more than one thing needed to help these children. We had talked about nutrition, food intolerance, the need for other professional help and perceptual movement in the schools. Norma had been so excited to receive confirmation of things she believed in.

Attempt 1, 1994

That same year, 1994, Norma made her 'Attempt 1' at setting up a movement program. She did this with her own Year 1 class and worked in with the other Year 1 teacher who also taught music. For two half hours each week she conducted a perceptual movement program with the two classes. They had a mixture of half from each class, one group doing movement and the other music. She had five rotating groups with helpers from Year 5. Later on a group of Year 2 children joined in too, making the groups a little bigger. Gradually parents came to help and the Year 5 students could be released.

Attempt 2, 1995

This year, two different things were tried. The perceptual movement program was introduced as one of the activities done on Thursday 'Clubs' day, for Years 1 and 2. Norma ran the program with another teacher, Mrs Kay Mitchell, who had worked with intellectually disabled children for many years and also with two or three parent helpers. (Kindergarten was done separately.)

Another result of our inservice session at Griffith in 1994 had been that a teacher from the Cootamundra/Junee area, Gaynor Walkins, went back and organised another inservice session for her area with Judy Bulluss and Peter Coles. Two of the East Griffith teachers attended this, one of them a Kindergarten teacher. She came back all fired up to run a perceptual movement program with the Kindergarten classes. Norma relates how she returned with understanding. "You have to have an idea of the philosophy and why you're doing it and what to look for."

Norma set out the program for the Kindergarten teachers. One weekend she got out her books – the Bulluss and Cole books, Jack Capon's and *Overcoming Learning Difficulties*. "I wrote down bits and pieces from everywhere and got them in some sort of order so I had five rotating groups. I included every memory activity I could find. The beauty of it is that the teachers who are doing it can see which kiddies are having difficulties."

Attempt 3, 1996
Time-tabling changes again. This year there were seven teachers involved as well as the music teacher who released one of the teachers at a time by doing music with the class. Each of the seven classes then had two teachers to run the half-hour movement program – one experienced at it and the other a sort of trainee. They used Norma's program to give them the structure and confidence they needed to get started. Wonderful parent helpers were used. In reality, the children were getting two perceptual movement classes a week because the music teacher included in her class a lot of rhythm, left/right and movement.

Attempt 4, 1996
Time-tabling again necessitated a change but by now the teachers in Kindergarten to Year 2 were all enthusiastic and experienced. Each class had their own movement program – seven classes. Parent volunteers helped. "They seem to enjoy helping with this more than with other school activities."

The Griffith teachers discuss the program
In a meeting after school we had a chance to talk informally. There was a real feeling of excitement. I looked back in my mind to my first visit where faces only looked interested and hopeful. Now the hope had become a reality.

"It makes them focus and concentrate on something."

"It helps them both in and out of the classroom."

"Kindergarten children had difficulty jumping over areas. I've spoken to a few parents about this since and they said, 'It's amazing. Kids usually jump puddles or they jump things.' But it's not always the case and it's really something you have to teach some kids in kindergarten."

"A lot of kids need stability."

"I noticed that a few in my group couldn't roll, they were terrible at pencil rolls. And the ones I thought would be good were the worst."

"It would be great if we could do it more than once a week but you just can't fit it in. The kids wish we could do it more often."

Doing movement every day
In this same teachers' meeting at Griffith, comments started to be made about doing movement in the classroom every day.

"Children don't do enough of these physical things any more. Everything is inside. That's why we need to do more movement activities than we ever did."

"Floor activity at the beginning of each day is important. I get my class to do neck rolls. It really helps. Finger play before handwriting. When we have a normal handwriting lesson, I put on each table a different activity – peg boards on one, play dough on another, chalk board, scrap paper, painting with a paint brush, using hands to manipulate the letter we are going to write. The play dough is really good for that. Then we do a formal handwriting lesson."

"Marg., with her music, incorporates left/right and rhythm. She does a lot of that."

"Then we have our sports afternoons."

The teachers started to see how this, as well, could be used for perceptual movement training – ball skills, basics for running.

Referral to other professionals.
It was all taking shape after only two years. Teachers no longer felt on their own and were beginning to call for help from other

professionals. The LD Support Group with Gerardine at the helm, had gone out and looked for all the professionals that were needed for learning difficulties. They found and inspired a physiotherapist, Prue Watson, a Mum who lived in the community. She took six months at least, of reading and going to courses to prepare herself. "I wasn't going to touch these little people without knowing as much as I could." She now has rooms in Griffith where she treats children referred to her by the Support Group and by the teachers.

A behavioural optometrist works at Albury and also one at Wodonga; and they have a parent who is an ophthalmologist who does small amounts of work for them. They had found a paediatrician in Griffith who had accepted their brain-washing about the importance of diet, but he has left. Now children have to go to Wagga, a trip of one to two hours away.

Griffith also had a gymnast who was knowledgeable about balance and coordination. A movement group was started up with referrals from the physiotherapist and this was going well. It stopped towards the end of the year but there are hopes it will start again. Schools could refer their more difficult problems to the physiotherapist and this gym group. There is also a chiropractor in Griffith who is interested in learning difficulties and "currently he is doing a course on cranial therapy". There are two speech therapists at the Community Health Centre and both of them are kept very busy.

A naturopath had also become part of the team and is helpful among other things with over- and underactive children. Gerardine is also working on the canteen committee to improve what is sold to the children. "I am the only member of the canteen committee who would like a healthful canteen."

It has snowballed

These were Norma's parting remarks to me. "I go to Gerardine's meetings and they're so keen, that little committee there. They do so much. They get all this information and wonderful speakers. Perhaps in your book you could point this out – don't put things in the too hard basket too quickly. Persevere. Two years ago we wondered if all this would ever happen, and it has snowballed. Teachers working hands on, can see it's great and they get talking and so on."

Expansion to Coleambally

The next day of this third visit Gerardine drove me to Coleambally to visit Kim O'Connor. She had been the Support Teacher at the time of my teachers' conference at Griffith. She had gone back to her own school from that seminar and had set up a perceptual movement program for her students.

Kim had done Reading Recovery four years before that. This developed into doing learning difficulties teaching where "I was assessing kids throughout the school. I was working with kids all the way from Kindergarten to Year 9 as a resource teacher in a support-type capacity. That's when I went to Barbara's course and started doing the 'left and right' program."

This program was to be available for the needy students in Years 3 to 6; those whom the teachers considered most at risk. The teachers had filled out my Questionnaire for Classroom Teachers (see Appendix 2) and, as a result of that, sixteen children were identified as needing help. Kim started the program with the intention of involving the whole group but soon found that the most needy nine were all she could handle.

The children talked about what name they would call this program. "They decided that if you wanted to catch a ball you needed your left hand and your right hand together. If you wanted to walk along the balance beam, you used your left leg and your right leg. So they called it 'left and right'. It's been called that ever since."

Kim also put in a submission to the Centre for Professional Development, Charles Sturt University, Wagga, for a mini-grant – and secured it. They bought equipment with this to supplement what they had, which was homemade. I liked the way she listed the aims of this program in her submission:

> "to develop self esteem in under achievers,
> to develop all aspects of Perceptual Motor Skills,
> to enhance and improve performance of students in classroom activities.
> (It is important to note that all communication skills, reading, writing, speech and gesturing are motor-based abilities.)"

Kim understood the importance of focusing on children's development as often as possible. She arranged the program so that they did 'left and right' four days a week with Kindergarten to Year 2 needy children. Each child was responsible for putting out a certain piece of equipment and then they cooperated in putting it all away. The whole thing took 30 minutes. They were also responsible for recording their own progress. Each child had a clip board with a pencil and as the stations changed each week they would get a new sheet and they had to tick off every time they had done one of the stations. (See Appendix for samples of two sheets – smileys for little ones and numbers for older students.)

With the older primary children at risk they incorporated 'left and right' into a general activities program for a bit over an hour including the High School. 'Left and right' was one of 15 activities to choose from Kim relates that "We found that the kids we had targeted chose the 'left and right' group for themselves. 'I want to go with Mrs O'Connor because I can't paint and I can't do anything with clay but I can roll on mats.'"

Kim wrote that "In 1994, I was invited as a guest speaker to the LD Support Group, to explain about the 'left and right' program and I took some of my 'homemade' equipment to show them."

Kim is a very organised lady and I was delighted to hear that they were setting up a data base. The school goes from Kindergarten to Year 12 so they are able to follow children through from five to eighteen years old.

The excitement radiating from Kim, as she was talking, had passed through the whole school. Even though they had had a change of principal each year since she had started the program, each one had been very supportive. The improvement in the LD children had inspired them all.

This year, 1996, Kim has become the Kindergarten teacher and I was able to watch her class doing 'left and right' while I was there. They had two Down's Syndrome children included in this program with the help of their teacher's aide. One of these Down's Syndrome children is in her Kindergarten class and the other in Year 1.

Kim says, "Their listening skills and ability to follow instructions has improved a thousand percent. I think it's just from taking them to the hall once a week and doing the 'left and right' program where they have to listen. Otherwise, they don't know what's going on and they can't follow. They want to listen. They love it."

Kim also applies her understanding of the need for daily activities to her class. Each day "we do some kind of gross motor development with these kids." They're out on the quadrangle doing hand-eye, running, kicking, "basically from what you said in your books, and other courses and books we've read such as Jack Capon's."

Apart from being the Kindergarten classroom teacher, during first term, Kim also took eight children from Kindergarten and Year 1, who were most at risk, for 'left and right' every day of the week. "We have an extra person on staff this year who works alongside the support teacher. She went out with the Year 1 teacher and the rest of the kids from Kindergarten and Year 1 to the quadrangle so that I could be left with the eight children." In second term there was a change in staffing with the support teacher taking a maths group so "unfortunately the only children doing 'left and right' at the moment are the kindergarten class." (September 1996)

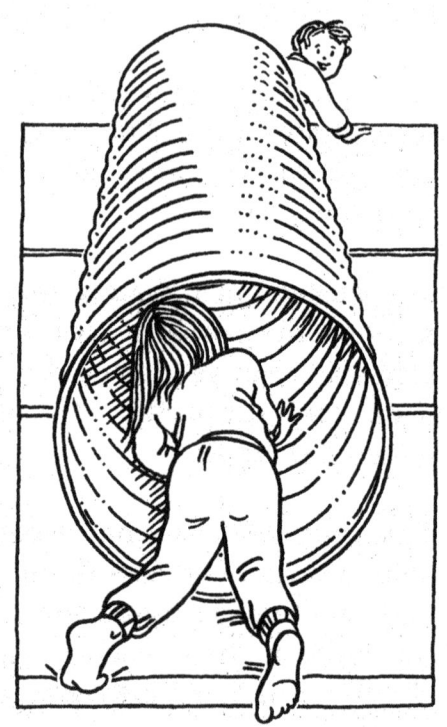

The community nurse was fascinated with what Kim was doing and invited the occupational therapist from Griffith Hospital to come and have a look. Kim said, "Holy Dooley, this guy knows what he's doing and here am I feeling my way, setting up these sorts of things and I thought, 'I hope I'm doing the right things.' And he was so impressed. He said that if he had a child in Coleambally, there's no way he'd drive his car all the way to Griffith Hospital to get the same sort of thing that we can offer at the school down here."

A network of schools

The next day I had the privilege of attending an inservice course, Smart Start with PMP, conducted by Judie Bulluss and Peter Coles from Victoria. This was the third time that they had been brought to this area since my seminar in 1994. I have described their teacher training program in Chapter 10.

These Smart Start with PMP courses had been arranged by Gaynor Waalkens, a local teacher with vision and drive, and I had an opportunity to talk with her for a short time at the lunch break. I asked her how she began her wonderful job of spreading the news about perceptual movement training into a network. "Attending the Inservice course that you ran, I got a lot of ideas and it started me thinking about how I look at children. I have always been searching for ways to improve what I was doing and how to best suit my students' needs."

Gaynor moved to Wallendbeen in 1994 and after attending the LD inservice course, decided to apply for funding available for Country Area General Component. To qualify for CAGC funding there must be more than one school involved, the focus had to be on literacy and numeracy and, if possible, the parent/school partnership enhanced. The Perceptual Motor Program, Smart Start, proposed by Gaynor, satisfied the CAGC panel on all counts.

The Smart Start with PMP Inservice was a huge success with teachers and parents from five participating schools, plus others, including preschool teachers. The network of schools was then put into place.

Wallendbeen Public School bought all the equipment. A teachers' aide was employed from the funding to organise the program, direct the volunteers and set up the equipment. This she carried in her 'ute' from school to school, travelling nearly 500 kilometres per week. Classroom teachers did the floor sessions, the evaluation and completed the language follow-up in their own classrooms after the program.

Preschools

Gaynor continues: "The program was also running in a preschool as a result of the Smart Start Inservice. A preschool teacher came to me at the Inservice and said she was interested in setting it up at her preschool but couldn't afford the equipment. I suggested to her that if the preschool committee would agree to pay their share of the expenses of the teachers' aide they could use our equipment. In Wallendbeen Public School the PMP became an integral part of our Kindergarten orientation program. All children who would be attending school the following year participated in the PMP. This has been very successful, establishing good home/school links."

Feedback

"The feedback from the five participating schools was fantastic – parents, children and teachers alike. All schools wanted to continue with the program in 1996, with another school joining in. Once again, in 1996, we ran the Smart Start Inservice course, training a new teacher's aide, as well as new staff members and parents." Gaynor moved to Hanwood Public School at the end of 1995, where they are in the process of implementing the PMP for children from Kindergarten to Year 2.

Griffith is in safe hands

You can imagine how impressed I was with the Griffith District after my three-day visit there. I couldn't even count the number of schools, let alone the number of children, that were now involved in perceptual movement training; and the number of strugglers that were now being identified and specifically helped in a number of ways. My latest contact with Gerardine was a phone call saying that a teacher from a Catholic school in Griffith had been in touch with her. She had missed the recent course and wanted more information. And so it will go on. Gerardine continues to be the link.

CHAPTER NINE
Movement for LDs in a state high school

People often ask if adults and teenagers with learning difficulties can be helped in this same way as children. Is it too late? Are they too old to be made ready to learn? The following story told by John Newberry, a teacher from Bundamba State High School in Brisbane, will answer these questions. The problem is the same no matter what age; the difference is in motivation. Young children can be enticed into exercises with games and encouragement. They also haven't failed for as long as older LDs. Teenagers with LD have usually built up a protective shell which masks the pain of failing – rebelliousness, not trying or getting kicks from doing other things, mostly anti-social.

In 1993 John, as the High School Resource teacher, among other responsibilities, had the job of working with 12- to 15-year-olds, a number of whom were already in trouble with the authorities. He had previously worked with all manner of LD students in High Schools, Technical Schools and Tafe Colleges. His own daughter had been remarkably helped by ANSUA in Brisbane (see Chapter 10) and John believed the same methods could help his students. They needed to have the causes of their problems addressed, not the symptoms. The foundations for learning needed to be laid, such as learning to listen, being able to use the eyes efficiently, and getting some measure of organisation into their lives; then, the symptoms of poor academic work could be addressed. And so, John set up a remedial program without reading, spelling, maths or handwriting lessons. The results speak for themselves.

One term to demonstrate success

"I was given one term to prove that it would be successful. The measure of that success was improvement in reading, writing and spelling in measurable quantities. The teachers in the school were asked to put down a short list of eight boys from Year 8 that they thought would benefit from special help with their reading and writing. A list of about 50 names appeared." This was reduced to eight. "I devised exercises that wouldn't be regarded as babyish. Quite a few things were challenging and fairly dare-devilish for teenage boys to do, such as, swinging from ropes, trampolining and climbing. They enjoyed what they were doing.

"The good thing that came out of that group was that there was sufficient development seen and the impetus to continue came from the feedback from parents. This started within three weeks of the beginning of the program. Parents said that their boys were far more tractable at home, had stopped fighting with Mum and chucking tantrums. They had started to succeed at doing something they enjoyed.

"That first program was six or seven forty-minute periods a week – about four hours work. They were supposed to be doing home exercise programs, as well, although I know this was spasmodic. There was enough progress in terms of the observable changes – self-confidence, self-esteem, physical abilities. I argue that the end products in terms of their reading and writing may not appear for 18 months or more. These were kids who either just sat in class and did nothing or kids who were thrown out every five minutes. No one else would have them. That group of boys are the Year 12s now. They have mostly done quite well. There are no genius scholars but they have got back into the mainstream classrooms and they have coped."

Building on success

John had enough encouragement to start off for another year with the same boys and a few more. They did the basic ANSUA exercises and he also "had some huge swings rigged in the big hall whose ceilings were nine metres high. We swung them in cattle lifting harnesses. There were trampolines and scooter boards and big balls. Part of the time was just play. Some of them lined up three of these big balls and went from one side of the room to the other on the three balls, rolling from one to the other without touching the carpet."

Several times during this period the parents heard that John might be moved to other duties or another school. Their objections, however, ensured that he stayed. The improvement in the teenagers became so obvious and so well known that parents were pushing to have their children admitted to the program and to stay longer. John could only handle at one time relatively few of the students who would have benefited. "We have seven Year 8 classes. In some of those classes over 50 percent have easily definable learning difficulties." In those early stages the size of the problem prompted him to have as many as 20 in a group at one time. This was too big to control.

Student contracts

This year, 1996, "I'm working with two groups for eight or nine periods each a week, eight in a group. The boys/girls are on contract and part of the contract is that they have to do six mornings or six afternoons of home exercises and they also have to come in two mornings before school at 8.10 a.m. rather than 8.50 a.m." But it only goes for five weeks. The school suggested that because there are so many students needing and wanting help that it was better to give more of them some success so they would want to keep going. John has put some students through two five-week programs. "Some really need two years of it and others have walked out after five weeks and done very well. There is a critical factor. When you get enough together then it (learning) suddenly takes off. There are some kids that you fight with all the way to get them to do what they don't want to do." Then John gives them an experience of overcoming something that they have been terrified to do. "It is the first time they have experienced personal success of overcoming fear. Then they really will do their home exercises and their sound therapy."

Sound therapy

John is also a qualified SAMONAS Sound Therapist (see Glossary) trained at ANSUA. He has incorporated sound therapy into the program, and the other part of the contract that he now makes with his students is that they have one twenty-minute period of sound therapy, each day at school. "The kids are driving me absolutely insane because they are at my staffroom door waiting to get on to the sound therapy. They know something has happened because their writing quality has improved. They like the sound therapy. They all have their own particular track they like the most. Many of them seem to feel that it is the only time when they are fully relaxed. Possibly more relaxed than when they are asleep. It's a very unusual sight to see a group of 12- or 13-year-olds lying quietly on a floor with their headphones on." When John started this five-week program, he tested five of the students so that he could measure the results and see what their improvements were in dictation. "They were averaging thirty-six mistakes on a page of dictation. This went down to six and seven mistakes and then an average of two."

Setting up the program
John does an initial interview with each boy (parents if necessary) of about 45 minutes. He gets them to do a simple sequence of movement and then several movements at the same time. Half of the interview is questioning and half is observing what they are capable of doing. He has an assessment sheet which enables him to find out the students' ability to lay out and place their work on paper, their dictation and mental arithmetic. He also has a handout, which he gives to parents, to explain the program.

The primary schools in the area which feed into Bundamba have also started perceptual movement programs. There was a teacher's aide in Year 1 who went around to the Infants schools and encouraged them to do this. One teacher is still doing it and her class is settled and doing fine. "All the other Year 1 teachers are tearing their hair out. The children can't sit still, they get up and walk around the room, yell at each other."

John feels that there are many things that could be done to improve the program, particularly in getting someone to work with him. Undoubtedly there will be growth and improvement each year. Some readers might feel they couldn't be as dedicated as John and the other teachers you have heard about in this book. The ANSUA staff, however, told me about another high school teacher who was only able to give his LD students lots and lots of marching. He maintains that this has made a huge difference to their ability to work in a classroom.

The brain is exploring the body
John shared a few of the activities he does with his students. "We do flip flops, homolateral and contralateral, ranging from very, very slow

ones so they become aware of everything that they touch – the feeling of their hands as they move over the mat, the pressure on the knees. They not only have to get the pattern right but they are exploring everything that their body is telling them, as they go. We do that with eyes open and then eyes closed. When they are starting on these slow flip flops they usually can't get it moving all together. They will move an arm, then a leg and then the head rather than doing the whole thing together smoothly. Then we do a moderate speed one and then a really fast one because when they are doing one really fast it is hard to maintain a pattern. (See Appendix 4 for description and illustrations of flip flops.)

Learning to do more than one thing at a time

John gives the following exercise, and others like it, to stimulate the different parts of the brain so the parts can work together at one task. This is necessary for efficient academic learning because classroom learning requires different sections of the brain to communicate and work efficiently together.

"As the students spread eagle on the floor on mats, you start giving them instructions such as, 'Move the index finger of your left hand in an anti-clockwise direction on the mat. Now, move the thumb of the right hand the other way, in a clockwise direction. Now move your right big toe backwards and forwards on the mat. Now move your left big toe sideways as you do it.' Usually as they start something new the old movements stop. But at the end of five weeks they are much improved and most can do it. They go home and get their Mum and Dad down on the floor and try and get them to do it."

An update on progress in 1977

In first term, John's ANSUA program became part of the curriculum but students could enrol by invitation only. Each student had ten 45-minute periods a week and they could stay in the program for one semester. Forty-five students were invited to participate out of 90 who applied. This curriculum subject is called the ANSUA Program incorporating SAMONAS Sound Therapy

By second term this year, four other teachers had finished their ANSUA training. This had been done over a period of eight weeks. They are currently able to enrol 65 students.

Training for high school teachers is the same as for any ANSUA teacher. The activities that are done, however, are adapted to teenagers' interests. You are free to call John at the school if you want any more information about ANSUA in high schools.

John Newberry
c/o Bundamba State High School
PO Box 311
Booval, Queensland 4304
Ph. (07) 3282 3011

CHAPTER TEN
Australian LD resources

The following resources are not meant to be an exhaustive list of what is available in Australia for classroom or resource and support teachers. However, they are the resources that I know about and can recommend. They are not listed in any particular order but only as a menu from which you can select and use what most seems to fill your needs.

ANSUA Developmental School Program (Queensland)
A New Start for the Underachiever (ANSUA), was established in Brisbane in 1976 as a registered charity by Jean Rigby, a qualified neuro-developmental therapist, teacher and SAMONAS sound therapist. Early on, she was joined by Maureen Hawke, also a neuro-developmental therapist, as well as a registered nurse, clinical nutritionist and SAMONAS sound therapist. They set up a centre in Paddington, Brisbane, where children needing individual help regularly attend with their parents. There they are assessed, given a home-based program and they return every few months for re-evaluation and program change.

Jean and Maureen also developed an ANSUA Teacher Training Course. This course has been given in many parts of Queensland, Papua New Guinea, Singapore, England, the Tamworth and Coffs Harbour areas in New South Wales and Bendigo in Victoria. Lectures have also been given in England, the United States, as well as Sydney, Newcastle, Melbourne, Perth, Alice Springs and throughout

Queensland. Unfortunately, Jean Rigby died suddenly in February 1997 but her significant contribution has been lasting and Maureen now heads up this vital organisation.

The strength of the ANSUA course is its concentration on helping teachers to get a vision of the 'big picture'.

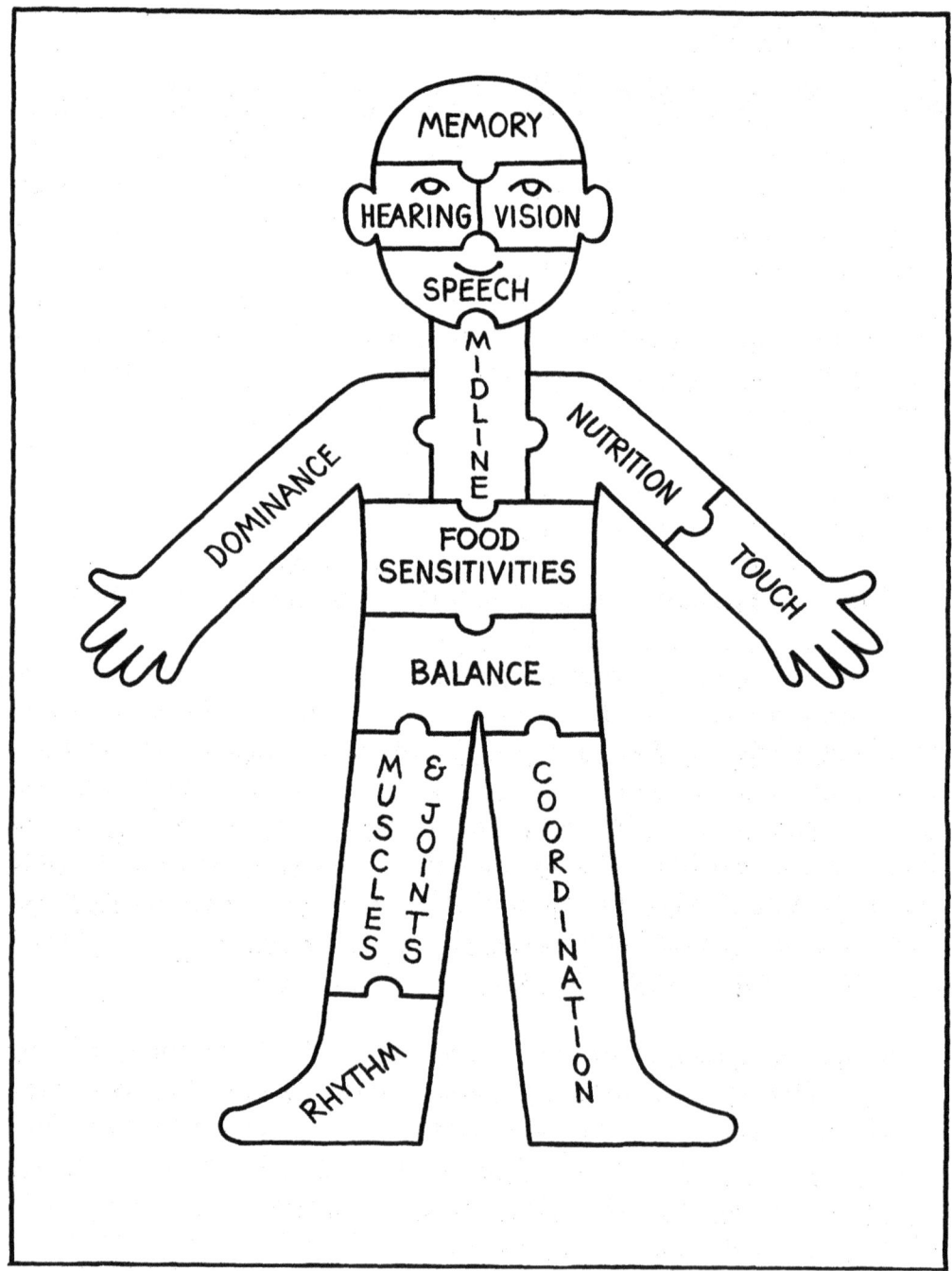

It is vitally important for teachers to get enough understanding to see that everything links up, the connection between physical development and learning. For example, the key role of touch is explained and how this tactile sense is linked to vision. Immature visual ability may be an indicator of an underdeveloped sense of touch. Similarly, improving posture may go a long way towards helping the visual and auditory systems. Again, the idea is to look at the total child.

Training seminars are in-depth in order to give this needed understanding, and may take place over five days. There are also courses with weekly two-hourly sessions over a period of eight weeks. It is possible to arrange a shorter introductory course for starters. It has been found to be most effective to have follow-up sessions after the teachers have been doing the practical activities with their classes for a period of time. Once the teachers catch the vision they become hungry for more knowledge.

The topics covered are:
- Neurological development of the child
- Role of reflexes in learning difficulties
- Neurological and other factors in ADD, ADHD
- Role of the visual and auditory systems in learning
- Nutrition and its role in learning and behaviour
- SAMONAS sound therapy

The physical program that the teachers learn to carry out with the children is very specific and is structured so that teachers know exactly what to do. The core of the program is done with the whole class for 10 to 30 minutes each day. It is done on the floor and needs little equipment. Plastic runners can be put over carpets. The first equipment to locate would be roller or scooter boards and overhead bars. Other activities are suggested, in addition, for variety.

The teachers report:
"For years I've been teaching children who were not achieving and I constantly asked, 'Why? Why? Why?'"

"I've now made the links between development and LD (as an early childhood teacher I had a solid understanding of child development – but had not previously made these links.)"

Help Your Class to Learn

"One of the first results from doing the program, and it happened fairly quickly, was a more attentive classroom with better behaviour."

Maureen says, "What ANSUA is trying to do, throughout Australia, is to educate people in child development and in ANSUA's methods, so that they understand how to help children with learning difficulties. In doing the ANSUA Developmental School Program with their classes, many more children will be helped. We find that once teachers get in and do the program, they don't ever give up because of the good results that they achieve in learning and behaviour."

Further research into the efficacy of the ANSUA Developmental School Program will be available in 1998. Inquiries can be made to:

Ansua Learning Centre
333 Given Terrace; PO Box 11; Paddington 4064
Ph. (07) 3369 1011   Fax (07) 3367 2242

Smart Start With PMP (perceptual motor program)

Judie Bullus and Peter Coles are two of the most efficient and practical people I have met and it was a delight to watch them at work, training a group of 60 or so teachers in their program at Griffith, New South Wales, in August, 1996. It was new to most of the teachers who were at this third seminar and a confirmation and a recharge for those who had been before. PMP reminded me of a pump. There was such a flow of energy and enthusiasm.

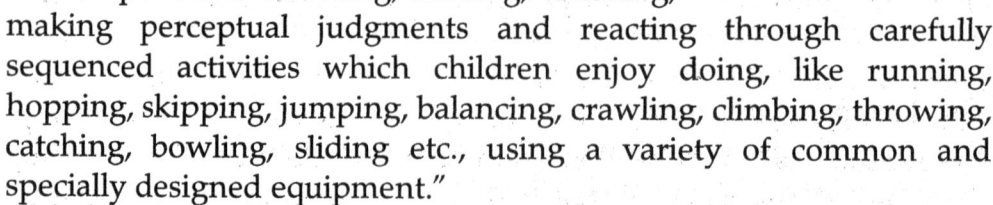

They say that their program "aims to give the child experiences in seeing, hearing, touching, making perceptual judgments and reacting through carefully sequenced activities which children enjoy doing, like running, hopping, skipping, jumping, balancing, crawling, climbing, throwing, catching, bowling, sliding etc., using a variety of common and specially designed equipment."

The PMP teachers' manual describes the background of this couple. They are both currently working as consultants for their perceptual motor programs and have come from the teaching profession, Judie originally from the music staff. "For many years she was coordinator of the Junior Department of Southmoor Primary School where she taught Prep and conducted a perceptual motor program which was open for visits by other teachers and parents from schools wishing to set up programs."

"Peter Coles was Principal at Southmoor Primary School and served the school in that capacity for 17 years. His qualification and training are in economics, mathematics and educational measurement. He came to motor programs by way of his dissatisfaction with the programs in schools that lead to many children failing to acquire the 'Access Skills' of reading and mathematics".

In conjunction with Deakin University Judie and Peter have completed a video explaining the perceptual motor program and its place in helping with cognitive learning.

Peter and Judie have brought the experience gained over 20 years working in perceptual motor programs to their publications: *Perceptual Motor Programs*, a manual for teachers (6000 copies sold); *Starter Activity Cards* (a set of 100 sequential and developmental activities); *Extension Activity Cards* (a further set of 100 sequential activities); *Language Follow up Activities* (photocopyable worksheets, allied to the motor activities, aimed at developing language concepts); and *Helper Handbook* (for parent helpers). The above is the resource material for the 'Smart Start' program.

They have been conducting Inservice Teacher Training courses for 15 years and have had contact with between 10 000 and 12 000 teachers, parents and support staff in Victoria, three tours of Western Australia, five to the Northern Territory and two lecture trips to New Zealand.

Judie explains: "The program itself is designed to be completed by *all* children for the first three years of school. They urge that the Prep (first formal year in school) program begins as close to the beginning of the year as possible, as that is the most important year. It is also essential that parents and volunteers be involved in the Smart Start program. In addition to the teacher, each activity station needs an adult, not only to supervise and keep the children on target, but also to give them adult language input. Good modelling is essential for language development. If you don't have lots of adult language input, then language development in the child is delayed. You can walk a child on a beam for ever, and it will make not one iota of difference to the general or learning behaviour of your class. If there is an adult there, saying, 'We're going from one end of the beam to the other', 'You're walking along the beam with one foot in front of the other and with your arms out and your head up and your back straight', it is only through that language that the children learn the perceptions of time and space for themselves. It's that, that is going to change the child, not just the walking on the beam."

Further information on the cost and content of inservice training and resource material can be obtained from

P. J. Developments
1 Albert Street, Mordialloc, Victoria. 3195
Ph. / Fax (03) 9580 0035

Movement for learning (Victoria)

A structured motor program for primary schools is available from Movement for Learning in Victoria. It consists of a manual outlining weekly changes of activities that form 20-minute class programs. These programs are designed to systematically follow normal movement patterns, from basic movements that enhance early levels of sensory and motor development to higher levels of function. There is a great deal of repetition within this structure. Interest and fun are added through warm-up activities and games. Accompanying the manual is an excellent 25-minute video which shows children from two schools doing the activities which form the 31-week program.

The program requires very little equipment so is easy to set up. There is a list of equipment at the beginning of each weekly program. Activities cover developmental movements such as rolling, spinning and both homolateral (unilateral) and cross-pattern stylised exercises.

Ideally the program is carried out with the help of parents. There are usually five different activities to be supervised, so four to five volunteers are required for each session. It is possible to run the program with the help of older students. It is suggested that two sessions a week is the minimum but that learning disabled students would benefit from four to five sessions each week. They might also be required to move through the changes to the activities more slowly, particularly at the beginning.

This excellent program has been drawn up by Pam Irwin, a physical education teacher working with Movement for Learning. This association was formed in 1972 by parents and concerned teachers to help children with delayed development and learning difficulties. The program was trialled in two schools for two years and was made available for all schools in 1989. In the seven years that followed, 375 programs have been sold to schools throughout Australia.

Movement for Learning carried out a survey of a cross-section of those schools who were using their program. They noted that whilst most schools using the program implemented it in the Infant Department, 40 percent continued its use into Middle and Upper Primary levels. The areas of most improvement were physical coordination, academic work and social abilities. It has been suggested to them that the academic improvement must have been significant for schools to be in a position to state that it was the Movement for Learning program that had altered academic achievement. Some other areas of reported improvement were confidence, willingness to attempt tasks, an increase in self esteem and children taking on responsibility for their own learning.

Preschools too
In 1995 a Movement for Learning manual and video were released for preschools. This is also a structured motor program designed to:
"improve coordination and body awareness,
improve sensory integration,
enhance visual and auditory skills,
build self-confidence through enjoyment and ability to move
prepare children for formal learning."

Movement for Learning
Box Hill,
Victoria 3128
Ph. (03) 9808 2993

Learning Foundations (Australia)

Ken and Marianne Johnson, in their pioneering work over the past 25 years with learning disabled children in the public school system of New South Wales, have started a new career. They have formed Learning Foundations in order to make some excellent resources available for teachers and to set up community LD service networks.

Ken Johnson, B.A.,O.A.M. was one of our first sources of inspiration and information about LD in the 1970s. I've known Marianne Johnson B.A.,Dip.P.E.,N.D.T., in the days when she was Marianne Coup and we first got excited about how movement helped LD children.

For the uninitiated in LD matters, a good introduction is the 20-minute video, *What Is Learning Disability*? A parent can take this to the school and say "Here is my child!" It can also be helpful to family members, as well as other professionals, in understanding LD.

Why Can't I Learn? is a seminar kit designed to be used by staff in schools. "It contains a seven-scene video tape, transparencies, photocopying masters and guidelines to assist the presenter. Each of the seven scenes depicts the way a student might show that they have a particular aspect of learning disability. Notes help staff members to consider how they might modify the presentation of teaching material and how to help students to present their work in ways that avoid some of the disadvantages associated with their condition. Teachers with no special education training can begin to improve the learning environment for their LD and ADD students."

Ken and Marianne have put together an excellent, in-depth, video course, with extensive notes, *Developmental Delay and Learning Disabilities*. Many of us took this course and it is very useful for those wanting more detail, such as resource teachers. There are also videos, available individually, taken from this course, on behavioural optometry, occupational therapy, physiotherapy and chiropractic therapy as they relate to LD.

The Secondary Emotional Factor, also taken from the above course, looks at a child's anxieties which lead to behaviour problems and stresses within the family. Ken knows of one man whose marriage was saved through this video.

Linear Sequential Organisation is a videotape of a one-day seminar, with notes. This is useful for teachers and parents trying to help their children organise themselves and their work.

The provision of LD services

Teachers who use perceptual motor programs are ideally placed to identify children who are more at risk. Their LD characteristics can be more pronounced. Such children would benefit from an individual diagnosis, followed by services of health and special educational professionals. For a number of reasons it is clearly difficult for our major public agencies, Departments of Health and Education, to meet these more demanding individual needs.

An alternative approach is for a community to establish and maintain its own LD service network. At the time of writing this, Ken and Marianne have developed a blueprint for just such a community-based service network. This blueprint will guide a community in how to set it up with the correct professionals, how to administer it, meet the costs and cope with the possible problems that will arise. You can contact Ken Johnson for this information and for any of the resource materials you may want to inquire about and purchase.

Learning Foundations,
2142 Gloucester Tops Rd,
via Barrington, NSW 2422
Fax / Ph. (065) 58 3191

The Ladder of Learning videos

Mary Lou Sheil and Margaret Sasse are a 'sister act' hard to follow. Mary Lou is a medical practitioner in Sydney, with expertise in the areas of nutrition, food intolerance, retained reflexes and SAMONAS sound therapy. Many of her patients are children with learning difficulties and she has been able, over the years, to use the many strings of her bow in helping them.

Margaret Sasse is the founder of Toddler Kindy Gymbaroo which is dedicated to, and highly successful in, helping children from six weeks to six years, develop and become ready to learn. There are 60 Centres which are in every state of Australia and in New Zealand.

Their programs include all the basic developmental activities that have been discussed so far in this book. Margaret also publishes *First Steps* an excellent child development quarterly magazine for parents. This magazine doesn't just make an ideal gift for the parents of a new baby but it would also help anyone understand more about the question of learning readiness.

All of this background is only a lead-up to telling you about the *Ladder of Learning* videos, produced by these two sisters. These five videos, starting with *The Importance of Being an Infant*, continue through each year, ending with *The Importance of Being Four*, which is really a documentation of learning readiness for school. From the back cover of *First Steps*, there is the following description. "These videos clearly show the important rungs up the Ladder of Learning to Integration, which is the launching pad for the rocket of academic learning. For the first time, parents and teachers can see these vital stages of early childhood development and understand their significance for achievement at school. Starring a delightful cast of children from babies to four-year olds, these five videos aim at academic achievement for all children, through an understanding of the foundations for learning established during early childhood."

Even high school teachers will find them informative because they will see three- and four-year-old children doing physical activities some of which their LD students never learned to do.

The videos can be obtained from:

Toddler Kindy Gymbaroo Pty. Ltd.
657 Whitehorse Rd.,
Surrey Hills, Victoria 3127
Ph. (03) 9899 1699
Fax (03) 9899 1788

Dr M.L. Sheil
80 Alexander St.
Hunters Hill, NSW 2110
Ph. (02) 9817 5202
Fax (02) 9879 6596

Improving literacy through motor development (West Australia)

One of the pioneers who understood very well the place of motor development in improving literacy was Rob Lefroy, a teacher in Western Australia. His trampoline sequence has been talked about lovingly, by many of us, over the years, because he was always so willing to share whatever he believed would help children learn to learn. The joy of his life was to teach and it is a credit to the forward thinking of the Western Australian Education Department that they asked him in 1962 to set up one of the first full-time remedial reading classes in Perth.

This was a withdrawal class for LD children who found the regular classroom to be, temporarily, too much of a struggle. They went into Rob's class for a period of months and there they became ready to go back to regular classroom work, able to cope and learn.

Rob developed a program of perceptual movement, including crawling, the use of a trampoline and ball skill development. He integrated this along with teaching methods adapted to their abilities to help these children become literate. His emphasis was in encouraging his students to become integrated, coordinated and with one side of their body as a dominant side. The results of all of this showed up in wonderful improvements in written expression, silent reading and handwriting.

The success of his work in educating children was honoured, among 75 notable graduates, by the University of Western Australia at its 75th Anniversary. In 1988, The Dyslexia Research Foundation of Australia, gave him their inaugural Award of Merit for Outstanding Educationalists. He has also been made an Honourary Life Member of SPELD (WA).

Rob's observations, methods and documentation of his success are all contained in a book he published in 1990, *Improving Literacy Through Motor Development*. The reading of this book and the following of its activities, which were used with Rob's students, could go a long way towards meeting the needs of LD students anywhere.

The book can be obtained from:

DYSLEXIA – SPELD
10 Broome Street
South Perth 6151
Ph. (09) 474 3494

A Sydney optometrist's books for classroom teachers

Charles McMonnies needs to be listed among those who pioneered the 'whole child' approach in Australia. He is an optometric practitioner, researcher, lecturer abroad and here, an Adjunct Professor, School of Optometry, UNSW, and lecturer in Paediatric Optometry since 1980. In 1972, he was one of the founders of the Sydney Threshold Clinic for LD children. I can remember that this clinic was one of the first places that Sister Yvonne Mary (my long-time friend and mentor) and I visited in our hunger for knowledge and it would have played its part in confirming our total child approach.

Charles McMonnies addressed the 10th Annual Conference of the Australian Early Intervention Association (NSW Chapter) in 1992 at the University of Sydney. His description of the thrust of this clinic is worth quoting here. "These children were given a comprehensive program based on the principles of neuro-behavioural dysfunction remediation (Ayres 1972, Morrison 1985) to encourage integration of primitive postural reflexes, improve muscle tone and proprioception, normalise tactile responses, establish body awareness, improve vestibular function, sensory integration and bilateral integration, and ability to cross the midline and to teach motor planning and sequencing skills."

McMonnies has also looked at the research that has been done and conducted some of his own into reversals and left/right body awareness immaturity. "Wearne and McMonnies (1992) examined 164 third-graders in three Sydney schools. They found a significant correlation between letter reversal tendency and reading disability for below average readers, but not for above average readers." (Australian Journal of Remedial Education, vol. 25 no 1 pp 8-9) *Reversal Prevalence and Reading Level Among Third Graders* was published in Aust. J. Rem. Educ 1992, 24: 15-18.

For our purposes here, how to provide help in the classroom, I needed to show some of Professor McMonnies' background so you can see where his booklet, *Overcoming Left/Right Confusion and Reversals: A Classroom Approach*, is coming from. Included with this brief and concise manual is the LRBA (left right body awareness) card which is also used in the classroom.

Referring back to the Pyramid of Learning, near the bottom, is the foundation of good body awareness. Professor McMonnies has gone through the literature and knows the essential, central place of movement in the process of learning. Movement provides the brain with the opportunity 'to get it together' and make those connections. He also shows that awareness of the left and right sides of our bodies is "the basis for left and right reference markers for easily reversed letters". (Early Intervention Paper)

In his first classroom book, Professor McMonnies describes the rationale and then a progression of simple classroom activities that any teacher of children in the early years of schooling, can use. His picture book, *Little Kim's Left and Right Book*, is used in infants' classes to introduce left/right awareness.

His books can be obtained from:

Superior Educational Publications
G.P.O. Box 2255, Sydney, Australia 2001
Ph.(02) 9264 6983 Fax (02) 9267 3741

The Learning Place

Pye Twaddell is a member of the Management Committees of PALD, the LD Coalition of NSW and SPELD NSW and, as such, is a part of the drawing together of the various professionals involved in working with LD children. She has her Masters degree in Education and is currently completing her PhD research in Early Childhood Education at the University of Sydney, Faculty of Education. She has many years of experience as teacher of the Perceptually Handicapped, in Early Childhood, LD and Reading Support Teacher, Primary Special Education, research and teaching with the Autistic Association, as well as 10 years of research developing her present resource material.

Pye's most recent materials include: *Evaluating Developing Learners* with assessment checklists for newborn to children aged six or seven; *The Kindergarten Screening* – a whole class school entry assessment; and *Teaching Developing Learners* "designed to answer 'where do I go from here?', giving immediate help to teachers and counsellors to translate assessed developmental and learning needs into appropriate classroom and home programs with individualised instruction across the curriculum." The 200-page Teaching Book includes: inservice information; the Ability Card Files with teaching strategies, activities and materials in the ability areas of Motor, Visual, Auditory and Communication; a 10-page Word Bank reflecting the predictable sound/symbol correspondences for decoding and spelling.

Kindergarten teachers would do well to consider *Kindergarten Screening*, which is the focus of Pye's PhD research, to validate a reliable Australian screening instrument. Over 750 children have been assessed in this longitudinal study and, for many, their subsequent school attainments have been followed through by classroom teacher surveys. The children are from schools in and around Sydney, as well as five schools in and around Dubbo (country NSW).

Screening categories are: Outside Motor; Fine Motor; Language; Paper/Pencil and Reasoning; and Personal Characteristics. The 50 screening items are standard kindergarten tasks requiring no special materials and are those for which children aged four and a half to six would typically be expected to be spontaneously successful at the independent level of function, identifying reliable information regarding the developmental and learning needs of each child. Screening takes place in the familiar setting of the children's classroom and can be completed for a whole kindergarten class within two hours. Results are then recorded and evaluated. The screening is given by the class teacher and three support staff, although need not all be given in one session. An inservice video is available.

Pye says: "The purpose of kindergarten school entry screening should be to inform referrals, programming, resources and, most important, instruction. Screening does not label. Each school entry kindergarten child should have equal access to instruction which accommodates his/her assessed developmental and learning needs."

For detailed information and inservice support material, contact:
   Pye Twaddell,
   The Learning Place,
   14 Chowne Place,
   Middle Cove, NSW 2086
   Fax (02) 9417 8309

Coordination Activity Programs (Department for Education and Children's Services, South Australia)

I haven't met Helen Short or Joan Crawford, but my valued friend, Judy Tankard, an insightful paediatric physiotherapist and a PALD member from its inception to her death in 1996, told me about their work several years ago. I knew, therefore, that they would be worth contacting. Joan Crawford and Helen Short, D.E.C.S. South Australia, are the developers of this program.

Helen responded to my inquiries by sending me the following three-stage program, an amazing collection of well thought-out activities.

Stage 1	Gross Motor	(children age 5 & 6) 1981, rev 1986
Stage 1	Fine Motor	(children age 5 & 6) 1986
Stage 11	Gross & Fine Motor	(children age 7 – 9) 1982
Stage 111	Gross Motor	(Upper Primary children) rev 1991
Stage 111	Fine Motor	(Upper Primary children) 1987

This program is for you if you want to target those 10 percent of underachievers who have mild to moderate motor delay. In addition, it will help identify those other few percent who have deeper and more basic problems so that they can be referred to specialist help.

The designers of this program developed it "to assist students who have difficulty in learning and performing motor skills. It has been designed to be used by teachers and school services officers intending to implement a coordination program with the support of parent helpers." They see a direct connection between the problems a child has with coordination and the general classroom skills of "writing, concentration, problem solving, following directions, attending to and completing tasks and listening."

The program's designers also recognise that there are other important areas affected. "Research in South Australia has shown that it is important to offer help as early as possible to avoid future social and emotional problems."

Helen and Joan recommend that "all five-year-old students be tested three weeks after beginning school, using the South Australian Motor Coordination test (SAM). This test can also be used for six-year-olds who are of concern. Students aged seven to twelve who are presenting difficulties are assessed using the Standardised Test Battery for the Assessment of Clumsy Children (Dr. S.S. Gubbay)

For each of the Stages of the program it is recommended that there be up to nine children to each half-hour session, three times a week, with one adult for each group of three children. They are tested again half way through a program as some children only need that much. They are also tested at the end.

Training videos and inservice training conferences are also available for those involved in conducting the program. I would like to make special mention of the Fine Motor programs as well as an extremely useful manual on *Developing Handwriting Skills*, 1994. Accompanying this is the Handwriting Wall chart which would be a useful addition to any classroom. These resources are available and very reasonable, to anyone in Australia.

Helen tells me that "80–85 percent of schools in South Australia, Government, Independent and Catholic, organise motor skill programs to help students with coordination difficulties and delay – 'Early Intervention'". It is usually done by a teacher support person with parent helpers.

For more information contact:

> *Helen Short,*
> *Department for Education and Children's Services*
> *Briar Road*
> *Felixstow, SA 5070*
> *Ph. (08) 8366 8814   Fax (08)8366 8809*

Working in a confined space

Maxine Anderson is a remedial teacher who works from her home in a small town in New South Wales, and I thought that her adaptability could inspire school resource teachers, working with individual students, who are somewhat cramped for space and find themselves limited in equipment.

"I live in an average-sized three bedroom home and since my

daughters have grown up and left home, I have taken over their bedroom as my study. My programs with the children always begin with some perceptual motor activities and my hallway gives me the most room to do this. My daily program notes might look like this.

1. Commando crawl up the hall – do a 4-piece jigsaw puzzle.

2. Wall walk back down the hall – arrange three or four pictures to make a sequential story. Tell the story. (Wall walk is done with the student facing the wall, two hands on the wall. Movement to the right is done by the left hand going over the right onto the wall while at the same time the left foot crosses over the right. If going the other way, the right crosses over the left. As the student does this he or she says 'left over right', or 'right over left', all along the wall in time to the movement.).

3. Collywobbles up the hall – arrange some word cards in alphabetical order. (Collywobble walking is done facing forward, crossing one foot over the other as you progress.)

4. Cross-pattern crawl – listen and tell me which word does not begin the same as the others.

5. Scooter board on tummy – obey three commands, 'clap three times, turn right around, stand on your left foot.'

6. Sit on scooter board and pull up the hall – read a row of arrows. eg 'up, down, right, left' etc.

"We might return to the study after this for balance and eye-hand coordination exercises. I usually have a piece of masking tape stuck diagonally across the room and along that they can walk heel/toe forward and backward, sidling along, tiptoe walk, small hops and jump from side to side. A practice golf ball hangs from my light fitting and this is used for hand/eye coordination, eye movement skills, laterality and dominance. I find that the children love this and frequently dart back to it for a 'play' between activities or while I speak with their parents.

"If I have a particularly restless student my back steps come in very handy. I write an 'r' blend (ar, er, or, ur, ir) on each step – or a vowel group (e, ee, ea, ey, ie/ei, y). I call a word involving one of the sounds and the child steps onto the appropriate step.

"For teaching directionality we have blind guided tours through the house. I take my student or he takes me. A left turn instead of a right turn can result in walking into a wall. For visualisation we sit in my study and the child gives me verbal directions to get to an area in my home.

"Not having a blackboard we use lots of scrap paper. Foam letters and a salt tray for spelling give children other ways of learning words.

"You can even use your kitchen. One of my students loved hot chips so we made them together. First he had to read the instructions: Choose large smooth potatoes, wash carefully etc.
"This practical exercise brought in sequencing, comprehension, language, fine motor, hand/eye coordination. We ate the results while playing a game of snakes and ladders, where three flash card words had to be read before climbing any rung.

"My kitchen vinyl tiles are the perfect surface for flip flops and for practising pat bouncing of balls."

Maxine has been so successful over the years because, I believe, she not only teaches reading, phonics, spelling, handwriting and written expression but she also prepares her students so they can benefit from her teaching. She uses a lot of movement and perceptual training and she incorporates games and her own individualised audio cassette tapes, wherever she can.

CHAPTER ELEVEN
The conclusion is that this is the beginning

Well, there you are! A veritable feast has been laid before you. It is all good food – it just depends on what you want or what you are able to take. There's even 'fast food' – take-aways with minimum fuss.

If you are not sure if you are hungry or not, you might consider the 'taste and try' method. You could do the exercises from the chapter on Oxford Falls found in Appendix 4 and just see what changes are brought about in even three months. Or you could buy the inexpensive Movement for Learning manual and video, and do that with your class for a year.

If you are the only one in your school who is interested in the significance of perceptual movement training, you might like to first spend as much time as possible in gaining a real understanding of this approach, so you will be able to make others eager to learn. Read Rob Lefroy's book, Gerry Getman's and *Overcoming Learning Difficulties*. If possible, attend an ANSUA course. Get in touch with teachers like Judith Hallin and Norma Marin. They were both so eager to learn and open to new ideas. Ask to observe a paediatric physiotherapist at work or an occupational therapist.

If there are other interested teachers from your school or area, you might very well decide to go straight to 'the mains'. The Smart Start teacher training program can be done remarkably cheaply if your school runs it, and enrolls other schools around you, to participate with you. The Smart Start program and ANSUA and any of the other items recommended in this book will change your teaching forever. Have high expectations and you won't be disappointed.

On the other hand if you are a resource, special needs and/or support teacher, you can't do better than selecting Ken and Marianne's insight in helping you get to the root of your children's individual problems.

Preschool teachers, teachers of the five-year-olds starting school as well as Infants school teachers could be very tempted by the normed screening of Gay Revie and Dawn Larkin. (See References: *The fundamental movement skill assessment manual*.) Pye Twaddell will also interest these teachers with her screening and the program which develops out of that screening.

One course, which is a set menu and which should not be missed by any teacher, are the five videos on child development produced by Mary Lou Sheil and Margaret Sasse. These provide a wonderful background knowledge about the neurological development of children, the last one, *The Importance of Being Four*, portraying all of the steps needed for readiness to learn.

What we have learned by putting this together

Certain things have been mentioned many times as we've worked and talked with teachers and volunteers, and as we've listened to others who have trained and inspired parents and teachers in this LD arena.

Start slowly
"Be sure there is at least one person in a school who really understands the total child approach, 'the big picture'."

Good preparation can mean quick results
You will begin to see results in a few weeks – improvement in concentration, self image and the ability to follow instructions.

Motivation
The essential ingredient is motivation. The person running the program must have the vision. Parents, volunteers and teachers will catch it as the children progress. They will need to provide motivation to the young children. Older children need to be challenged to 'see the

light' for themselves. "Once you can get a kid to catch the vision and get motivated, then you've got them. They'll do the program, even the boring crawling, and come out tops at the other end."

Combine exercise and language
Another essential ingredient is a great deal of language. "Adults have to program the language in, before we can expect it to come out. Body awareness can be developed by an adult talking to children about what movements their bodies are making, such as 'Your left foot is in front of your right foot on the beam'" Children being encouraged to talk while they move has a magic ability to integrate the brain. Adult volunteers are an indispensable part of this approach.

Every day
It has to be done as often as possible. This is why preschools and schools are the only place where all children can be prepared for learning. Very, very few mothers can find an extra half hour a day, for months, to work with one of their own children who has LD. But something can be done every day in schools. Some classroom teachers, like Judith Hallin, fit it in themselves. In other schools, the music teacher does her important part laying foundations through music and rhythm. Sports or physical education teachers have the opportunity to lay these same foundations, as they are being laid in South Australia, by opening up the possibility for all children to be ready to participate in sport, thus automatically laying academic foundations. It is also helpful to understand the Pyramid of Learning, and include rolling and crawling with children.

Daily eye tracking
One thing a classroom teacher can most certainly do is five minutes of daily eye tracking with the whole class. (See Appendix 4.) If they get red, watery eyes or can't follow the ball, send them for specialist help.

Specialists can help
We must use the skills of all the necessary professionals in helping these children. Let us no longer be islands unto ourselves.

How little we know of each other
The most astounding thing that I learned, while putting this book together, was how little we know about each other in Australia. So few

had heard about the wonderful work that others were doing. Sometimes this was true, even in the same state. So, hopefully, communication can be increased, where we share what we know, with no professional guardedness, with no desire to prove that 'I have more answers than you'. Let's honour our fellow workers and let's have the expectation that they will be able to teach us something we didn't know.

The Internet may possibly be a tool we can use to enable us to get to know each other better and to share our knowledge openly. When those of us who care so much for those with LD get hooked up on Internet, we will all, both in the country and the city, be able to access all of the things that are going on – research, successful programs, Australian-normed assessments. We can begin to talk to each other. Those who are just starting out can find someone to help them.

So, it's over to you now, to share any other resources for classroom teachers that you know about that will prepare LD children for learning. These resources can be advertised on the Internet or I would be pleased if you would like to tell me about them.

Mrs Barbara Pheloung,
4/1 Tower St., Manly 2095 NSW
Fax (02) 9907 7049

GLOSSARY

Apraxia
The inability to plan motor movements

Auditory perception
The learned skill of acquiring meaning out of what is heard.

Bilateral integration
The integration of the two sides of the body and the two halves of the brain so that the body functions efficiently as one whole.

Brain biofeedback
A device to help those with Attention Deficit Disorder to control their attentional mechanisms. Electrodes on the head feed into a biofeedback machine enabling them to monitor their brain waves and adjust their behaviour accordingly.

Brain imaging techniques
These modern techniques allow us to not only get detailed pictures of the anatomy of the brain but also allow us to study the uptake of glucose while different tasks are done. This enables us to see how well each area of the brain is being used for each specific task.

Cognitive learning
Learning that comes from using the thinking part of the brain, as in reflection, perception, apprehension and observation.

Cross-pattern/contralateral movement
Movement that requires opposite arms and legs to move together.

Directionality
An awareness of direction (left, right, up and down) which develops after we automatically know the left and right sides of our own body.

Educational Kinesiology (EK)
EK enhances our ability to learn by improving right and left brain

coordination. It draws upon the knowledge of brain process, remedial educational techniques and some of the principles of oriental medicine.

Evoked brain potentials
This measures how a particular brain handles a stimulus, allowing us to see if there is delayed or dysfunctional processing.

Feldenkrais Method
A system of learning through body awareness and movement.

Fine motor
The ability to control the small muscles of the body, primarily in the eyes and hands, necessary to successfully perform such fine motor tasks as handwriting.

Glue ear
This is a congestion of pus and mucus inside the tubes of the ear drum which impairs hearing. Children are more susceptible to this condition because their tubes are narrower and don't drain as easily. The liquid needs to drain away so that the ear drum can be filled with air through which sound waves can pass easily.

Gross motor
The ability to use the large body muscles (arms and legs) in a smooth coordinated manner.

Homolateral /unilateral movement
Exercises where the movements are together on the same side of the body (eg left arm, left leg and head to the left).

Hyper-
A condition of any of the sensory systems which allows an excess of sensory stimulation to the brain.

Hypo-
A sluggish sensory system which doesn't allow enough of the sensory stimulation to reach the brain.

Hypoglycemia
Not enough sugar in the blood to meet a person's energy requirements.

Laterality
Referred to here as an automatic awareness of the right and the left sides of our own body.

Midline
This is an imaginary line which divides a person's body in half. It acts like a wall in babies but it disappears at around three to four years through normal play and movement. When it persists after this time it interferes with the development of coordinated activity where the body has to act as a whole organism. It also slows down academic work when both sides of the brain should work easily together.

Moro reflex
This is a primitive reflex for the purpose of survival. When a baby feels threatened or startled he throws his head back, his arms forward, arches his spine and straightens his legs so he can get his lungs full of air to cry for help. This develops into the adult startle reflex at around six months.

Motor planning
The ability to process and plan a movement.

Neurological organisation
This is the process by which a human being achieves his/her potential, subject to environmental forces.

Normed
A test is normed if it is able to compare a student's performance with others the same age or in the same grade.

PALD
These are the initials for the Sydney based Professional Association for Learning Difficulties

Primitive reflexes
These are involuntary movements which all babies have during their first few months. They assist in the birth process, some help protect the baby and others get him moving until he learns to control his own movements.
When these reflexes are no longer needed they normally disappear.

Proprioception
Information from the muscles, joints and tendons to the brain.

SAMONAS Sound Therapy
(Spectrally Activated Music of Optimal Natural Structure)
Uses very specialised CDs which are listened to through headphones. It is used to treat those with dyslexia, learning or behaviour problems, attention deficit disorder, autism, developmental delays as well as

adult hearing problems. It was developed by Ingo Steinbach who describes it as "micromassage of the muscles within the middle ear preparing the organism for further stimuli". This results in the stimulation of the total brain.

Sensory integration
The integration of all of the information received through the senses (eyes, ears, skin, muscles, balance, taste, smell), so that the body can automatically and efficiently use it for movement and learning.

Sequencing skills
An awareness that there is an orderly arrangement in the nature of things and that there are causes and effects.

Spatial relationships
The awareness of the relationship of symbols and objects to each other in the space around the person who perceives them.

SPELD
The initials for the organisation called Specific Learning Difficulties Association.

Tactility
The feelings from the skin sent to the brain of temperature, pain, pressure.

Unilateral movement
See homolateral/unilateral

Vestibular
Refers to the part of the brain that helps the body adjust to gravity. A mature vestibular system promotes good auditory and visual communication, sorting messages like a postal service.

Visual perception
The learned skill of making sense out of what you see.

APPENDIX

1. ASSESSMENT AT THE BEACH HOUSE

LD children were assessed at the Beach House, our therapy centre in Manly, by a paediatric physiotherapist and a resource teacher. Many of these children were also assessed by other professionals and a record of all these results was kept for each child. Certain physical characteristics seemed to keep repeating themselves so we decided to put the results of 187 assessments done in the early 1990s into a computer. Each of the behaviours was put into one of three categories; no significant problem, some problems and significant problems.

The figures recorded below include only those characteristics which were significant problems. Sometimes the children could find a way around these and compensate, but it usually resulted in them having to try harder. For example, the first characteristic recorded was the ability to concentrate. Seventy-seven percent of our children could not do this. Another significant difficulty that almost three-quarters of the children had to cope with was in the lack of integration of the two sides of the body. The two halves of the brain were slow in learning how to work together efficiently. Seventy-three percent couldn't use their body naturally in a coordinated, cross pattern manner. Seventy-one percent still had the significant evidence of a midline wall which should have disappeared when they were around three years of age. Seventy-one percent were neither fully right-sided nor fully left-sided. We haven't included in this appendix those who had some immaturity, rather than significant immaturity and those who were at the correct level of development for their age. The bar graphs, however, have included these figures.

Poor concentration 77%
Eyes not working together easily 30%
Inaccurate awareness of space around them 46%

Poor ability to remember what has been seen 46%
Those who have had glue ear and nasal problems 51%
Inability to remember a normal number of instructions 67%
Significant vestibular immaturity 63%
Clumsy because of inadequate messages from the
    muscles and joints to the brain (proprioception) 55%
Significantly immature messages from skin to brain 41%
Very immature awareness of own body 58%
An imaginary line still dividing the two halves of body 71%
Poor coordination 73%
Don't have a clear leading or dominant side of the body 71%
Find it difficult to understand others' language 33%
Find it difficult to express themselves 29%
Significant difficulty in seeing an order or a sequence 73%
Very immature understanding of the length of time 58%
Significant difficulty with reading accuracy 45%
Poor comprehension 32%
Much difficulty in sounding out words, or word attack 56%
Significant problems with spelling 51%
Great difficulties with mathematics 53%
Handwriting very stressful 51%

2. TEACHER CHECKLIST FOR LEARNING DIFFICULTIES

If you are worried about the performance of any students in your class, observe them, and fill out the following questionnaire.

NAME _____ Birth date _____ Class _____

	YES	SOME	NO
1. Is disruptive and overly talkative.			
2. Is overly quiet, tries hard with little success.			
3. Poor memory – learning something one day and forgetting it the next.			
4. Poor posture and tires easily.			

Help Your Class to Learn

	YES	SOME	NO

5. Needs to prop himself up after writing or reading for a while.
6. Can't naturally hold a pen/pencil properly without thinking about it.
7. Bumps into and knocks things off desks
8. Reluctant to join in on games and sports.
9. Terrified of climbing and afraid of heights.
10. Little natural sense of danger.
11. Loves rough and tumble games and sometimes a bully.
12. Hates being knocked, poked or touched and seems to exaggerate small hurts.
13. Seems generally more immature than others.
14. Doesn't mix well with peers.
15. Poor eye contact.
16. Dislikes ball games.
17. Makes crooked columns and can't place work on paper as nicely as others.
18. Copies inaccurately from the white/blackboard.
19. Sensitive to outside glare and fluorescent lights.
20. Eyes too close to the book when reading.
21. Moves whole head when eyes move back and forth while reading.
22. Poor at noticing things that other children notice.
23. Finds it hard to hear what the teacher says when there is normal classroom noise.
24. A 'daydreamer' or switched off.
25. Hates loud noise. (Some tend to talk loudly to drown out the noise of others).
26. Instructions have to be repeated.
27. Phonetics (sounding out words) is difficult.
28. Can't tell a logical fluent story to the standard of others in the class.
29. Speaks ungrammatically.
30. Great difficulty learning the alphabet and multiplication tables.
31. Always last or late; finds it hard to learn school routine.

Appendix

Extra questions for those seven years of age and older

	YES	SOME	NO
32. More trouble than others learning to tell time.			
33. Appears to be ambidextrous.			
34. Reverses letters, numbers or words. ie 'b' for 'd', 'was' for 'saw'.			
35. Has to think about which is his own left and right sides.			
36. Can't do more than one thing at a time, ie write and listen.			
37. Often misses the points of jokes and finds reading comprehension and arithmetic problems hard.			
38. Doesn't know where to start a classroom task.			
39. Seldom finishes his work.			
40. Can't organise himself, forgets to bring sports' gear, can't find things in school bag.			
41. Still has some articulation problems.			

SCHOOL ACADEMIC RESULTS

Reading _____

Spelling _____

Maths _____

Handwriting _____

SELF ESTEEM/ SOCIAL _____

_____

EYESIGHT
  When tested _____

  By whom _____

  Results _____

HEARING

When tested _____

By whom _____

Results _____

Interpretation of questionnaire

This is a screening. If you see a concentration of 'yes' answers in a group of questions it can indicate that further investigation needs to be done. The areas covered by different groups of questions are:

Questions 1 to 14 cover physical development. A number of 'yes' answers indicates the need for perceptual movement training, or even a visit to a paediatric physiotherapist or occupational therapist.

Questions 15 to 22 cover visual functioning and visual perception. May need to be referred to developmental optometrist.

Questions 23 to 27 cover hearing and auditory perception.

Questions 28 to 29 are concerned with language.

Questions 30 to 32 are to do with an understanding of sequence and time.

Questions 33 to 36 can indicate a child is immature in the integration of the two sides of his body.

Question 37 refers to comprehension and possibly visualisation.

Questions 38 to 40 targets the ability to organise.

Question 41 asks about speech articulation.

3. STUDENT RECORD CARDS

JOHN SMITH

Problems: Body awareness, sequencing (can only remember two things at moment), craves vestibular, language

1. Vestibular (Basic Bounce on trampoline) *Overcoming Learning Difficulties pp. 157-161.*
1 2 3 4 5 6 7 8 9 10 11 12 13 14 15 16 17 18 19 20 21

2. Flip Flops
wk 1   2   3   4   5   6   7   8   9

3. Body Awareness
wk 1   2   3   4   5   6   7   8   9

4. Punching bag
wk 1   2   3   4   5   6   7   8   9

5. Bilateral Activities
wk 1   2   3   4   5   6   7   8   9

6 Tactile
wk 1   2   3   4   5   6   7   8   9

JANE PEABODY

Problems: Vision, craves tactile, body awareness

1. Flip Flops
wk 1   2   3   4   5   6   7   8   9

2. Vestibular (Basic Bounce)
1 2 3 4 5 6 7 8 9 10 11 12 13 14 15 16 17 18 19 20 21

3. Body Awareness
wk 1   2   3   4   5   6   7   8   9

5. Bilateral Activities
wk 1   2   3   4   5   6   7   8   9

5. Tactile
wk 1   2   3   4   5   6   7   8   9

6. Eye exercises
wk 1   2   3   4   5   6   7   8   9

4. ACTIVITY CARDS

Even if no other exercises can be managed, regular daily flip flops and crawling can change a child forever. I have encouraged adults to do this with excellent results from only a few minutes daily. It is important, however, to follow the directions and illustrations carefully.

Flip flops, crawling and creeping

These are to be done each session for the whole year, if at all possible. Those children who find it more difficult than the others, can be encouraged to do some at home. Each stage should be done for four to six weeks, depending on improvement. Some children will be efficient in some stages and need only four weeks. Others will need longer.

Unilateral flip flops

Sister Yvonne recommends that the flip flops be done in three stages until this is easy, before doing it as a continuous movement.

a. Child lies on stomach, head turned to the right looking at her right thumb. Her right leg is bent at right angles at the knee. Her left hand and arm are down by her side and her left leg is down straight.

b. Child says 'down one' as right arm and leg go slowly down the side together.

c. Child says, 'head one', as head turns to look to the left.

d. Child says, 'up one', as left leg and left arm are slowly moved to the position that the right arm and leg had, with eyes looking at left thumb.

Child continues 'down two', 'head two' etc for agreed number of times, starting with six and increasing the number gradually.

After a few weeks, or when this is easy for the child, it can then be done as a continuous movement. As one arm and leg go down, the other slowly comes up and at the same time the head turns. The object is to keep in contact with the floor, do it slowly with leg, arm and head coming to their destinations at the same time.

Appendix

1. Unilateral flip flops

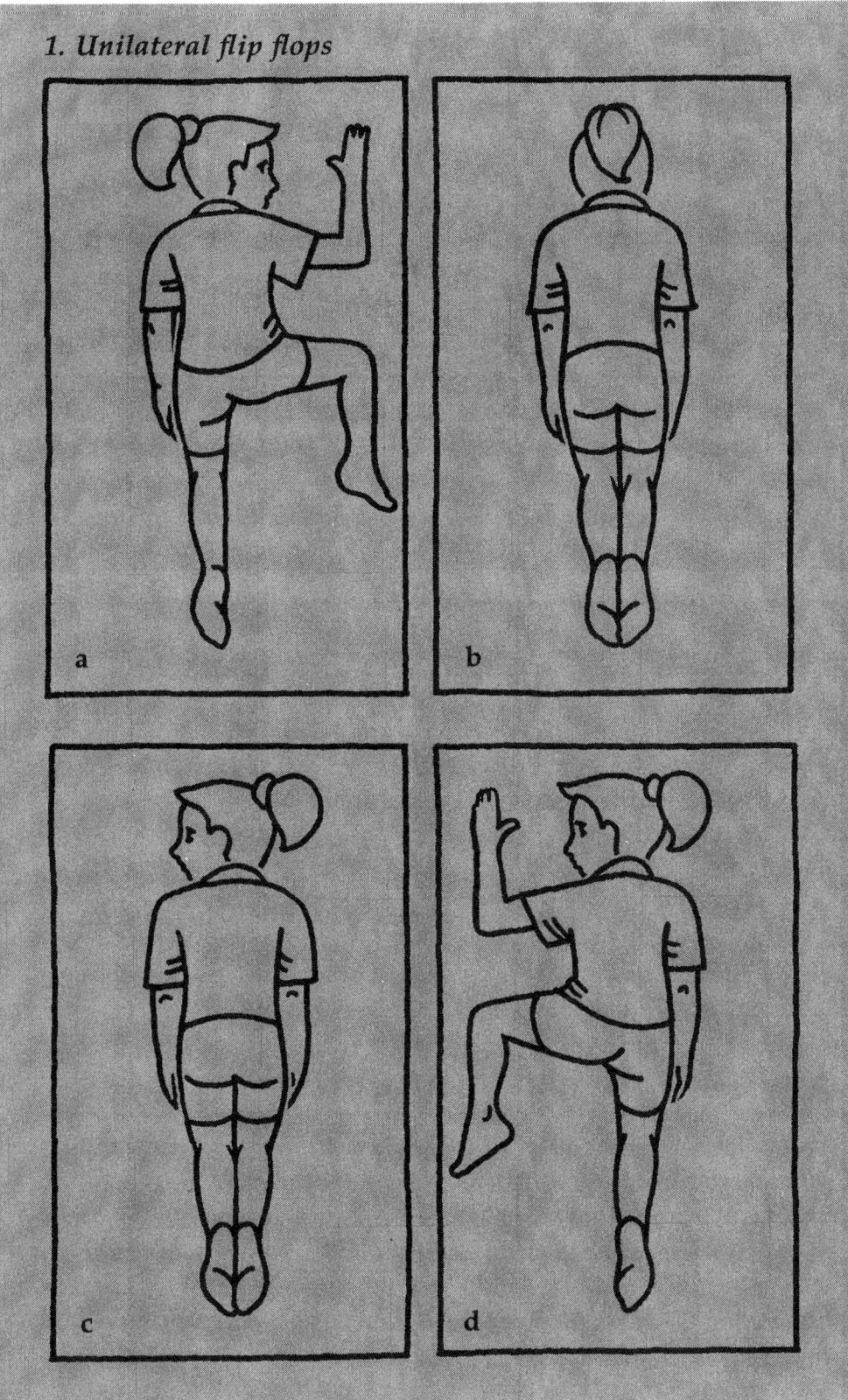

2. Cross-pattern flip flops

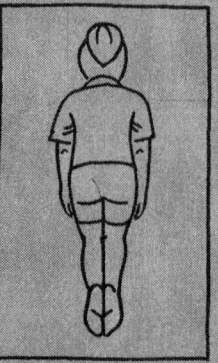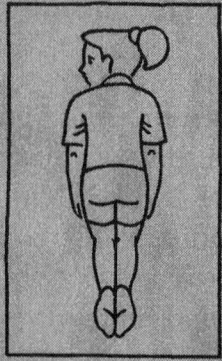

Begin with head turned to the right, right arm bent with the thumb across from the eyes. This time the left leg is bent while the right leg is straight. The left arm is down the side. The student may well need to do this in three separate stages first as with unilateral flip flops.

3. Unilateral stomach sliding/crawling

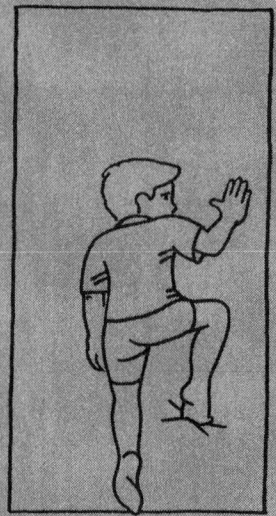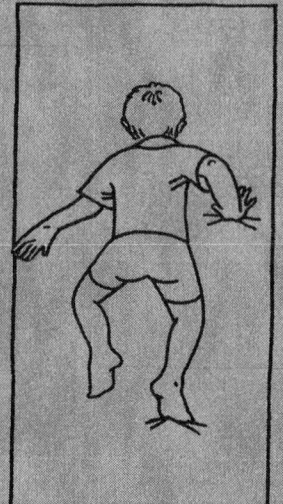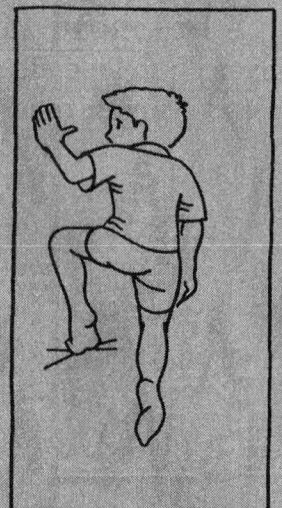

This is the same position as for the unilateral flip flops, but the child slides forward with each change, by pressing down with his hand and digging in with the toe of his bent leg as it straightens. The child may need specialist help in learning how to do this. He may also need your help to keep the arm and the leg, not only moving together, but completing the movement at the same time. Counting, "one, two" rhythmically and with emphasis can help.

Appendix

4. Cross-pattern stomach/sliding crawling

Cross-pattern flip flop position (2) with sliding movement as in (3). The child may find it difficult to move the opposite arm and leg absolutely together at the same time. It can make a lot of difference if an adult helper counts with him.

5. Unilateral crawling on hands and knees

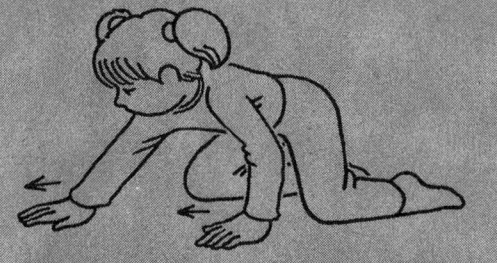

Child is on hands and knees, dog position, with hands and knees shoulder width apart. The right knee and the right hand move together and hit the floor at the same time. The fingers of the hand point straight ahead with the thumb in. The knees are lifted while the feet and toes are dragged along the floor. The head turns and eyes look at each hand in the forward position. If the child can't do all these together at first, start with what he can do, and gradually add the rest.

6. Cross-pattern crawling on hands and knees

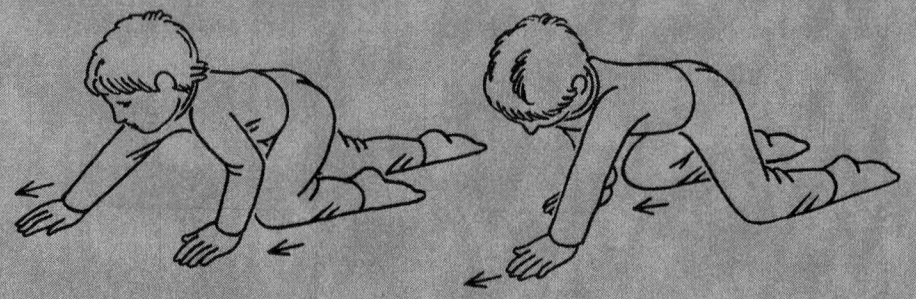

The same things apply as for unilateral crawling, except that in cross-pattern crawling the opposite arms and legs move together.

7. Cross-pattern walking

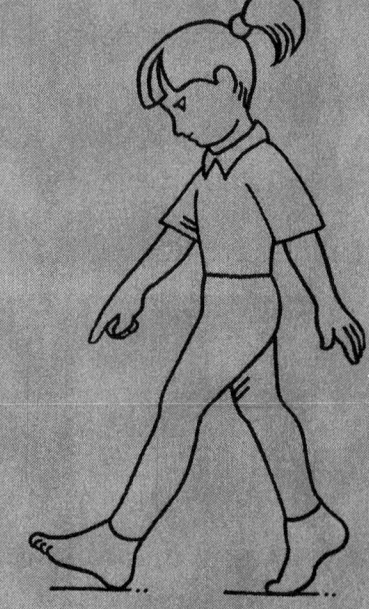 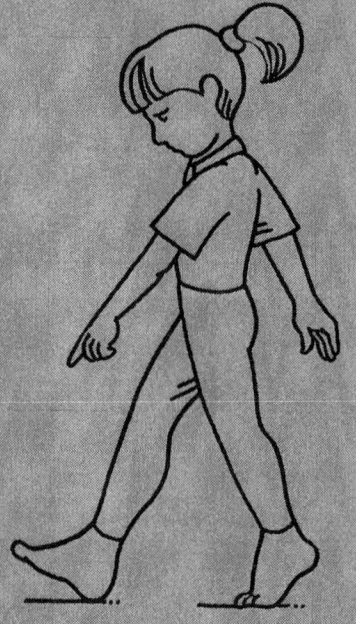

This is deliberate and fairly slow. As one foot goes forward the child looks at it and points to it with the index finger of his opposite hand. His head moves from side to side as he looks at and points with his finger to the toes of each forward foot.

In this last term, as well, give the children variety by getting them to change back and forth from unilateral to cross lateral movements. This is a great brain challenge.

Appendix

Body awareness

It is very important to talk about left/right in each session and only move on to more challenging exercises as the child becomes fully confident in each activity.

1. Point to and name parts of the body. Talk about left/right.
2. Look at self in mirror. Point to and name parts of the body.
3. Volunteer calls out name of body part. Child points to it on his own body and repeats name. (Eyes open and then eyes closed).
4. Roll along room keeping body straight (eyes to focus on a point while rolling). Do in each of the following ways:
    a. arms above head
    b. arms at sides
    c. leading with head
    d. leading with shoulders
    e. leading with hips
5. As 4. but with eyes closed.
6. Lie on back in barrel. Gently rock from side to side. For variety, do in each of the following ways:
    a. arms out in front
    b. arms at sides
    c. repeat while lying on stomach
    d. roll along room in barrel.
7. Copy positions made by volunteer.
8. Gloves, shoes.
    a. talk about which goes on right and left. Try them on.
    b. draw around hands and feet.
9. Give quick commands to child to 'touch left shoulder', 'bend right knee', 'stick tongue out to left', 'with left hand touch right ear', 'with right knee touch left elbow', 'with left foot touch right calf' etc. If this is accurate and automatic then go on to 10.
10. Follow left/right directions, eg 'five steps to left, three forward, six to right'. Increase number of instructions as child is able. Continue until he is sure of left/right directions.
11. Blind guided walk. This can be done with pairs of children, or by the volunteer with the child, one person blindfolded. This is a good test to see how automatically the child can follow directions. "Take three steps forward, turn right, take two steps, turn left, side step three to the left." These can be increased and varied according to the child's level. The partner prevents crashes into things, if necessary.

Bilateral activities

In weeks 1 and 2:
1. Lying on scooter board, push off from wall with two feet.
2. Lying on scooter board, pull along hallway using two arms.

In weeks 3 and 4:
3. Jump two feet together along room.
4. Jump two feet together along room while clapping hands in time with feet.

In weeks 5 and 6:
5. On stomach, pull body along mat using two arms together.
6. Jump from side to side over a line or tape on the floor, using two feet together.

In weeks 7 and 8:
7. Bounce on mini-tramp, hands on head, count to 20.
8. Bounce on mini-tramp, clapping hands, count to 20.

In week 9:
9. Skip with rope, jumping two feet together.

Eye exercises

Two minutes of eye tracking done every day would improve all students' ability to use their eyes efficiently in the classroom.

1. Each child holds up his index finger or a pencil, at arm's length and watches it as he moves it in a circle, up and down, side to side and diagonally with his right eye. His left hand can cover his left eye.
2. The same using his left eye.
3. Then with both eyes.
4. Child watches ball hanging by a string at eye level as he moves it in a variety of directions.
5. Child hits hanging ball with a cardboard tube held in both hands. The tube can have a line drawn around the middle of it so that the child can hit the ball first on one side and then the other – 'left, right, left, left, right'.
6. Near and far. The child practises focusing alternately at card or book held at reading distance and then at blackboard or wall chart. A different letter or word can be read aloud each time the eye focuses.

Punching bag, pillows, bean bag chairs

Activities with this equipment helps with body awareness, handwriting and visual ability and sequencing. Encourage children to punch firmly and with gusto with their fists.

In weeks 1 and 2:
1. Punch bag 10 times with right hand, counting aloud at time of impact.
    a. Repeat with left hand
2. Punch bag several times with right hand saying *'right, right, right, right'* at time of impact.
    a. Same with left
3. Punch bag several times with alternate hands saying *right, left, right, left, right, left* etc.

In weeks 3 and 4:
4. Punch bag with right hand once, saying *'right'*, then once with left, saying *'left'*.
    a. Punch bag with right hand twice, saying *'right, right'*, then twice with left saying *'left, left'*.
    b. Punch bag with right hand three times, saying *'right, right, right'*, then three times with left saying *'left, left, left'*.
    c. Then put this together: *'right, left'*; *'right, right, left, left'*; *'right, right, right, left, left, left'* naming the appropriate hand at the time of impact.

In weeks 5 and 6:
5. Same as number 4 but do up to four with each hand.

In weeks 7, 8 and 9:
6. Volunteer calls out 'right' and 'left' at random and student listens and responds to each call by punching with the required hand and saying which hand it is.
    a. Volunteer makes up a sequence of calls such as 'right, left, left, right' and after the call the student performs punches in the correct order, naming the hand he uses as he uses it. Volunteer increases difficulty as student progresses.

Trampoline/rebounder

Recommended as a start to all therapy is the basic bounce sequence described in *Overcoming Learning Difficulties* on pages 157-161.

Safety first
If a school or a community group plans to use a trampoline for therapy or exercise they should contact their local trampoline association first. The Trampoline Sports NSW address is PO Box 497, Glebe 2037. Phone Cassandra Ellis, 9660 3355.

Using a trampoline with care
It is relatively easy to become a Level O instructor and then on to Level 1. This not only explains the safe way to include trampolining but also how to avoid the consequences of accidents for your association. The NSWTSA Inc have also put out a Trampoline Coaching Video which explains and illustrates Levels 1 to 4. But even if your group does not want to do trampolining as a sport but rather as therapy, there are many useful safety hints offered. The instructor has the right to enforce safety. Some hints follow:
- Untapered springs give more control.
- Toes should be stretched when going up.
- There should be four spotters around the trampoline at all times.
- Knee drops are no longer recommended; instead suggest landing on hands and knees.
- A bell can be tied under the centre of the trampoline to reinforce where the centre is.
- Socks should be worn so toe nails don't get torn off.

It's very important to warm up and to cool down.

Once you are a Level 1 coach, you can become a member of the trampoline sports association in your state and take advantage of sports injury insurance.

Alternatives to the trampoline
1. Sit on a rebounder with legs crossed and gently bounce. The child can be engaged in a variety of other activities at the same time.
2. *Overcoming Learning Difficulties* has a number of other vestibular activities listed on pages 102–106.

> ## Tactile stimulation
>
> Stimulation of the skin is one of the most basic ways children get information about the world. It can be helpful for overactive, tense children who are unable to concentrate. Some children may crave skin touch while some others will dislike it. If a child's card says that he or she dislikes touch, then you must be very careful not to touch them without their permission. Either way, they would benefit from the following activities as often as possible.
>
> ### *Tactile bath*
> This is a collection of a big variety of things that feel different, such as soft pillows, rough blankets, velvet, feathers, bits of wool and materials, clean old paint brushes etc. They can all be put in a big container or on the floor in a corner. Children spend the time crawling under and through and talking about the things they feel.
>
> ### *Pretending to wash or paint*
> Children pretend to wash or paint themselves. Volunteers can say the following: "Take this wash cloth and pretend you are washing your legs very slowly. Tell me what you are doing as you do it. The front of your legs, slowly, down the back of each leg, your right foot, your left foot, now your right arm slowly down from the top of your arm to your hand. Then each finger. The same with your left arm and hand. Then each shoulder and your head.

5. ARTICLES ON LEARNING DIFFICULTIES

The following articles, by the author, for Oxford Falls Grammar School Parents Newsletter were written to encourage parent awareness of learning difficulties and what they could do to support their children and the school's Individualised Learning Program. They can be copied, or parts thereof, and used, as long as their source is acknowledged.

Individualised learning program at Oxford Falls Grammar School (October 1993)

Thought for the month
Educating children is something like making gravy. You have to get the early stages right.

Help Your Class to Learn

Year 1 groups start

This term sees two Year 1 groups starting to participate in our perceptual movement program, laying the foundations for future learning. Like the older groups, they will be doing specific movement activities which include such things as coordination and balance. They will also do fun things which give them practice at listening more closely and looking more accurately. Organising their movements and things around them will also help prepare them for learning.

A number of these basic skills are needed for academic and social success. If a child has an under-used or under-performing area of the brain, we are treating it like a weak muscle. Practice and exercise make it function better.

Extra tutoring in academic work at this stage is not the answer. Tutoring attacks a specific subject; it doesn't tackle the basic reasons why a person is having trouble with that subject.

There will also be changes this term with the Year 5 and 6 groups. Work with these students will be done individually rather than in the group sessions we have done before.

Mrs Z., volunteer

One of the first to volunteer to help with the program, Mrs Z., came every week in the first term to help with the making of equipment. Then, when the first groups started in second term, she was a mainstay for the Monday groups.

After struggling with a learning problem all her life Mrs Z. says she knows the frustration involved. She agrees that the correct approach is to get rid of the blockages at an early age. "This frees them to learn. The blockages also affect their personalities and how they cope with life. When the blockages are removed, interacting with other kids becomes easier and they are able to be fulfilled within themselves and achieve things."

Mrs Z. has also had her son on a sugar-free diet with wonderful results. His concentration has become much better and his reading has dramatically improved. She is happy to talk with any other parent about these and other exciting results.

Appendix

How on earth do you cut out sugar?
This was surprisingly easy, according to Mrs Z., once she got down to the business of adapting her regular recipes and looking at new ones. She has also found sugar-free sweets. At the moment she is compiling a number of sugar-free recipes and is about to launch into milk-free recipes.

What do jigsaws teach children?
Jigsaws can be a fun family activity at home and are especially good for children with learning difficulties. There are jigsaws for all ages but just be sure that you don't provide ones that are too difficult or too easy. Jigsaws teach the following things:
How to organise a task.
A sense of achievement.
Fine motor control – useful for handwriting.
Eye-hand coordination – a skill needed for handwriting.
Practice at making sense out of what is looked at – useful for reading.
Space and time language – useful for mathematics.
Develops the sense of touch – needed for handwriting.
Provides the opportunity for the two sides of the body to work together and gives the child the chance to cross over the imaginary midline of his body, with the arms and the eyes.
Encourages the visual skill, important for later academic learning, of seeing *the whole* from its *parts*.
Teaches sequencing – a skill needed in everyday life and in studying.

In helping children put a jigsaw together follow these steps:
1. Lay out *all the pieces* with *the right side up*.
2. Look for *four pieces* that have *two straight edges joined at a corner*. Teach them the word, *'right angle'*. Soon they will be able to look for four corners or for four right angles.
3. Place the pieces roughly in position. Try to work out which pieces would go at the *top, bottom, right side* or *left*.
4. Look for and sort out all the pieces with a straight edge. Try and place them in position to make *a border*, joining the four corners. Again, decide on top, bottom, right and left.
5. Lastly, take the *middle* pieces, one at a time, study *the shape* and look for a similar shaped *hole* in which to fit it.
(All the words in italics help to develop language. From Frances Francis, physical education teacher at the Beach House, Manly, NSW.)

Individualised learning program at Oxford Falls Grammar School (November 1993)

Thought for the month
"There is no such thing as a genius. Some of us are just less damaged than others." From *The Conscious Ear* by Alfred A Tomatis.

Kinder screening
At the beginning of the year we did a kindergarten screening created and compiled by Pye Twaddell B.A.,M.A. This was a 'first' for us and we did it because we wanted to know the children's maturity level in the different areas of development such as motor, language, looking, listening and fine motor.

Just recently we re-did the screening in order to measure our success. These screenings give us the opportunity to plan better and to be objective in our measurement. Individual scores are not necessarily significant, because a child might feel a bit sick on the day, or have his ears blocked or the assessors might also vary one from another, in their judgments of a child's performance.

However, the overall results are interesting. Pye has screened a number of schools in her work of standardising her tests. She said that our school can be very proud of our children's achievement during the year. Over-all success rates are quite high compared to other schools. (The fact that we have such a high percentage of English-speaking students is one reason for this.)

Another observation that Pye made was that in schools which had a structured physical education program, done daily, kindergarten students measured were better than ours at rhythm, strength, ball playing etc. This might be one of our future aims.

The volunteer, Mrs M.
One of our most dedicated volunteers with the program is Mrs M. She saw new hope for her children when our program was first introduced at a parents' meeting at the beginning of the year. In the past she has seen remedial work done, unsuccessfully, with her two children so her positive interest and willingness to learn were very encouraging. When the new approach of first laying the foundations

for learning was explained, both she and her husband felt immediately that it was relevant and offered an opportunity to help them.

Mrs M. has seen a noticeable improvement in her daughter's self-confidence and willingness to try new things. Although she has been on the program for just over one term, Mrs M. feels that her own new understanding of her daughter's difficulties has helped to change the way she deals with her. Moreover, the girl no longer thinks of herself as a failure but knows she only has difficulties to get over. Her mother's dedicated work with the groups has given her almost as much as she has given to others. She recommends that everyone who suspects a problem with learning in their children should get onto it early.

Eye muscle exercises

The following exercises should be done daily;. they say that this can prevent you from ever needing glasses. The exercises would certainly lessen the strain that classroom learning puts on young eyes.

This is from a video made by Freedom Vision, obtainable through Bethany Allridge, PO Box 81, Albury, 2640 NSW.

The first four exercises should be done standing up. Palming takes place in exercises 5–9. It is done by placing the hands together, palms over the eyes, with the base of hands resting on the cheek bones.
1. Shoulder roll – only the shoulders going slowly around – 10 each way. (Arms should be relaxed.)
2. Nodding – gentle nodding well forward and backwards 10 times.
3. Head turns to look over each shoulder, left and right, slowly, 12 times each way.
4. Chin circles. Imagine you have a pencil on your chin and draw big circles with it gently. 12 each way.
5. Moving eyes up and down as far as they will go, keeping head still. Three sets of six times each. Palm between each set for approximately three to five seconds.
6. Moving eyes horizontally as far to left and right as possible, without moving head. Three sets of six times with palming briefly between.
7. Diagonals. Move eye-balls up to the top corner of the eye on one side and down to the bottom corner of the eye on the other side, slowly. Six times for each diagonal for three sets each, palming in between each set.

8. Make circles with the eyes, keeping the head still – big and smooth. Four circles both ways and three sets of each with palming.

9. Finger focus. Hold your finger in front of you at normal reading distance and line up an object at the other side of the room. Alternately, look at one and then the other. Do two sets, ten times as quickly as you can.

Individualised learning program at Oxford Falls Grammar School (February 1994)

Thought for the month
Breakfast protein for the brain is like petrol for a car.

The end of the first year
A number of people have asked us if we have seen results yet from our movement program at the school. It is too early yet, of course, to see academic improvement in Years 1 to 5 as they have only been doing the program for less than one and two terms respectively. Year 6, however, have been working on it for nearly three terms. Even though we all knew, from the beginning, that would not be enough time to effect all the improvements that can be made, there have been some exciting changes. This is doubly significant when you realise that, with these older children, who have failed to achieve to their potential for so long, there are often emotional barriers and resistance to therapy.

Among the Year 6 children there have been instances where reading has improved more than double the expected rate, where mathematics has finally made sense, where the ability to organise their work has noticeably improved and so on.

As far as the younger children are concerned, I have heard a number of spontaneous comments from the volunteers. "I've noticed a real improvement already in their ability to do the activities." "Their confidence is growing." " They tell me when I forget to do part of an activity." "They love it and don't want to miss out on anything."

This younger age, when children are eager to try, is the easiest time to lay the foundations for learning. 1994 will be an exciting year also. If we have as good a group of volunteers as last year, nothing's going to stop us. We hope that they will come back, and that more, who can make a commitment to coming an hour or more a week for a year, will join the team.

Protein for breakfast
Everybody needs protein for breakfast if they want to be able to work to their best during the day. This is particularly true for children's learning. When I am helping with the trampolining with Years 5 and 6 children in the morning, it is obvious whether they have had protein that morning or not.

Several mothers have asked in what foods, other then meat, protein can be found. The Natural Food Catalog by Vickie Peterson has been a mine of information.
Alfalfa has a very high protein count and alfalfa flour and cereal can be added to other grains, to make one of the best sources of protein.
Buckwheat, rice and whole grain rye have a good protein content.
Oatmeal porridge with milk.
Cheese is a complete protein and one of the least expensive.
Eggs have a balanced protein which the body uses easily.
Baked beans on wholemeal bread are good.
Peanut butter and other nuts.
Beans and peas provide a good cheap source of protein – roughly double that of cereals and higher than that of meat, fish and eggs.
Soya beans are exceptionally high in protein.
Sesame seeds and sprouts are also excellent sources.

Individualised learning program at Oxford Falls Grammar School (July 1994)

Thought for the month
The mixture of fat, sugar and caffeine makes chocolate about as bad a food as we could have. This thought came from the Hyperactivity/Attention Deficit Disorder Association newsletter.
Ph. (02) 9411 2186 for further information.

The trouble with handwriting
The harder we try the harder it gets. This is certainly true of handwriting and it's very logical once you understand the way

our joints in our bodies work. We have two kinds of joints – moving and moveable.

Moving joints are meant to move freely and, in order for this to happen, the muscles around the joints must be relaxed. Moving joints are in the fingers, shoulders, elbows, knees, ankles, toes and hips. Tension makes the movement more stressful so, the harder that someone tries to do handwriting, the harder it is to do.

Moveable joints will move only if the muscles around them tense up in order to move them. Moveable joints are found in the spine. If the back or neck is hunched or bent then there must be tension in those muscles. And so, if the back is bent, muscles will be tense and the movement of the moving joints of the body will be more difficult.

While doing handwriting the back may be twisted to the side. For example, a student may sit on his legs as they are twisted to one side with spine twisted. This means that the spine has to turn again so that the shoulders are more or less over the hips, thus making the shoulders slanted. Other students will almost lie on one arm on their desks as they write. In these cramped positions there is little chance of relaxed and easy hand movements.

Moving joints and posture
Moving joints are required for handwriting so it is essential that muscles be relaxed; these joints can then move freely without tiring the body.
- If the spine is hunched over the desk, muscles are tense.
- If the spine is twisted, muscles are tense.
- If a child is trying terribly hard, muscles are tense.
- If the messages going to the brain from the skin, muscles and joints of the hands are inadequate, then the child is confused and tense.

To avoid the muscles tensing children need to be encouraged to sit on their bottom bones with their heads easily balanced above their bottoms, their shoulders and necks relaxed and their bottoms back in the chair with feet flat on the floor. They need to become aware of their hips so they can tilt their bodies forward over the desk from the hips, keeping their torso relaxed.

Children should write with big easy movements for as long as they want with large letters. Once they are relaxed enough in their movement they will be able to make their letters smaller. They should also play plenty of games with their hands and arms so they become aware of all the different ways their joints are able to move. These could include games with string, the church with the steeple and people, jacks or bones, pick up sticks, shadow play and lots of clapping games.

If children don't have enough awareness of touch in their hands they will benefit from plasticine and clay. If their muscles and joints don't give them enough information then it would benefit them and also be fun to do familiar activities with their hands while blindfolded.

How teachers can help
For ten minutes after each extended period of handwriting children could lie on the floor while the teacher reads to them. This is also good after working on a computer.

Do not tell students to try harder, to sit up straight or keep their shoulders back as these will only make them tense. *But rather* "Balance over bottom bones. Feet flat on the floor. Shoulders and neck relaxed. Bend from hips. Bottom back in the chair."

Little hand games can be played which help the children become aware of finger movement and joints. When children are learning their alphabet, for example, they can make the shape of the letters with their fingers. Older children could learn to talk with their hands as deaf people do. For all ages clapping games are excellent such as clapping on different parts of the body in a certain prescribed sequence, or clapping out Pease Porridge Hot, blindfolded.

How parents can help
Parents can certainly help improve their children's posture. It is not always necessary to remind a child by telling him; the best way is to do it correctly yourself. As well, a gentle hand on your child's shoulder could remind him to relax and stop tensing his muscles. If a child has not established a dominant side of his body (that is, if he doesn't use the same hand for all tasks) then a parent can encourage this child to doodle and draw with different hands so the body can decide which

one should be the leader. When it becomes obvious to the child that one hand is more skilled than the other, then that hand should be the leading hand, or the one used in all tasks as the dominant one.

Playing with plasticine, clay, mud and sand are ideal activities for children who don't like cutting out and drawing. Games of marbles, string games, jacks, yo-yos and many others will all prepare them to be good hand writers. Playing musical instruments is also excellent but for some this is too hard. These children need to have more sand, plasticine and mud first.

Holding the book with the non-writing hand
Students of all ages need to be encouraged to hold their book with the non-writing hand if they don't do it naturally. A person who is integrated, whose two sides of the body work well together, will just naturally hold the book while the other hand writes. Both sides work cooperatively in a different way to do the same job. Children who don't do this naturally can be reminded by touching or moving their arms. It may help also if they realise that their brains will be able to work more efficiently if they do this.

Credit and thanks for the information about the muscles and joints of our bodies is given to Geoff Morrison, Osteopath and Steve Jones, Alexander Practitioner/Body Therapist both of Neutral Bay, Sydney.

Individualised learning program at Oxford Falls Grammar School (August 1994)

Thought for the month
A child may hear all right but be unable to listen well.

Listening
Everyone has to learn to listen. We are given the ability to hear, well before birth. And learning to listen starts then as well. Newborn babies recognise the sound of their parents' voices at birth.

Babies and toddlers learn to listen through moving. As the head moves, the distance between each ear and a sound varies in length, giving slightly new messages to the brain as to the position of the sound. Babies also learn to listen by making their own noises and by listening to others, particularly adults.

The ears are important for other development because a major part of the brain's stimulation comes through ears. They influence balance and our movements. They permit us to learn language, to speak eloquently and to sing in tune. Our ears are even involved with our eye movements as we read and our arm, hand and finger movements when we write. And they also shield us from hearing what we don't want to hear, including the sounds of our own body. Children who are distracted by every noise in a classroom are sometimes thought to hear too well. Wrong! They are not good listeners. A good listener can focus on what he or she wants to hear even with background noise.
Why is it that at least half our children who have learning difficulties are also poor listeners? You can be sure that they don't want to miss out on what is going on around them. Nobody would choose to be a poor listener although we might sometimes think that this is the case with our own children.

One of the most apparent causes of poor listening is recurrent ear and nasal infections which stop the ear from hearing what it heard the day before, in exactly the same way. These confused messages are fed to the brain and particularly affect language development.

Watching television continually gives children too much low frequency buzzing which dulls listening. Another problem is that the sound of television sets is often of poor quality. As well, most television programs have a great many short changes of scene so that a child doesn't have to learn to listen for any length of time.

Another deterrent to learning to listen occurs if young children are asked to sit or not to speak for long periods of time. (Poor listeners need lots of movement and language no matter what year they are in at school.) Teachers and parents can take children's natural play as a guide for their own teaching of them. In children's play there is so much language and movement even if a child plays alone.

To summarise what action parents and teachers can take
1. Do whatever is necessary, quickly, to unblock nasal and ear passages. A diet free of dairy products can be all that is needed.

2. Let each child in a family have time to talk and be listened to.
3. Limit television watching.
4. You should speak with good rhythm, clear articulation and lots of expression. This will help almost as much as anything else.

The view of one of our volunteers
Mrs P. helped with the groups last year and this year and her warmth and love of the children has been a wonderful help. She jotted down a few of her thoughts about our program.

"I have worked with a number of these children since they started the program last year and have seen them move forward in terms of concentration and ability. At the start of the program, the children were often negative or frustrated at being unable to complete certain tasks. Now they attack them, knowing they can succeed and the overall behaviour patterns are calmer and more positive. I have been fortunate not to be forced into the workplace myself and so have time to spend here. I have also seen, not just at our school, the exasperation and frustration of parents dealing with a child's difficulties in certain areas. It is great that we can give them help in overcoming these problems. The rewards of seeing a child become more confident and well-rounded is quite satisfying."

6. PARENT INTERVIEW FORM

The following information will be treated confidentially. It will help us understand the needs of your child and plan appropriate activities. Please fill this in and bring it with you to the parent interview.

NAME _____ Date of birth _____

ADDRESS _____

_____

_____

_____

PHONE _____ Hm _____ Bus_____

Appendix

PARENTS' NAMES_____

BROTHERS AND SISTERS with their ages_____

At what age and how did you first notice his/her LD problems?
_____

SOCIAL
   Does your child make friends easily? _____

   Does s/he have a best friend? _____

   Are there problems on the playground?_____

   What are his/her special interests and hobbies?
_____
_____

DIET, EATING HABITS AND ANY PRESENCE OF FOOD SENSITIVITIES
_____
_____
_____
_____

EDUCATION
   What schools has student attended and what grades were done in each school?
_____
_____
_____

   What age did s/he start kindergarten? _____

What comments did teachers usually make about the student's progress at school?
_____
_____
_____

Was much school missed and if so, why?
_____
_____

Does student like school? _____

Behaviour at school? _____
_____

Has student been assessed for learning difficulties before?

When? _____ By whom? _____

Results? _____

List any therapy or remedial help that has already been given.
_____

Has your child seen a school counsellor? _____

Results? _____
_____

Has speech been assessed by a speech pathologist? _____

By whom? _____

Results? _____

Has speech always been clear? _____

Tell logical story? _____

Does s/he get instructions and directions confused? _____
_____

Appendix

MEDICAL HISTORY

Does your child have any health problems? _____

Medication? _____

Did or does student have sinus, nasal or ear problems and at what ages?

_____

_____

Has sight been tested? _____ At what ages? _____

By whom? _____ Results? _____

Has hearing been tested? _____ At what ages? _____

By whom? _____ Results? _____

PHYSICAL DEVELOPMENT

Did child crawl in a cross-patterned manner and for how long?

_____

Was, or is your child more clumsy than peers? _____

Before 5 years of age did s/he enjoy colouring, cutting out and crafts?

_____

Good at sports? _____ Ball games? _____

Does student use left or right hand or some of each for: writing?

_____

Brushing teeth? _____ Combing hair? _____ Eating? _____

Cutting out? _____ Ball throwing? _____ Batting a ball? _____

7. RESULTS OF WORD RECOGNITION READING TEST, 1977 (Judith Hallin, Queensland)

Judith tested and re-tested the following children after seven weeks of doing her ANSUA movement activities. They are not from her class but from the next class who joined with her class in doing the program.

			GAIN IN MONTHS
Child 1	No improvement between one test and the next. "This child plays up so much each time we go to do the exercises, and in general, that we moved him away from the group when we do them. We are working out ways to improve the situation."		0
Child 2	Chronological age (12 July)	9y 3m	
	Word Recognition Age(12 July)	6y 10m	
	Word Recognition Age(30 August)	7y 2m	4
Child 3	Chronological age (12 July)	9y 6m	
	Word recognition age (12 July)	10y 5m	
	Word recognition age (30 August)	11y 1m	8
Child 4	Chronological age (12 July)	8y 11m	
	Word recognition age (12 July)	8y 4m	
	Word recognition age (30 August)	9y 4m	12
Child 5	Chronological age (12 July)	8y 8m	
	Word recognition age (12 July)	9y 9m	
	Word recognition age (30 August)	10y 10m	13
Child 6	Chronological age (12 July)	9y 6m	
	Word recognition age (12 July)	10y 10m	
	Word recognition age (30 August)	11y 7m	9

Average gain in Word Recognition over seven weeks was 7.6 months. These children gained more than a month in word recognition for each week of ANSUA movement activities.

Appendix

8. STATION SHEETS

Station sheets for children in Movement Program at Coleambally. The children carried these with them as they went to each station so the parent helpers could see each child's chart. The ones with the smileys were for the younger children.

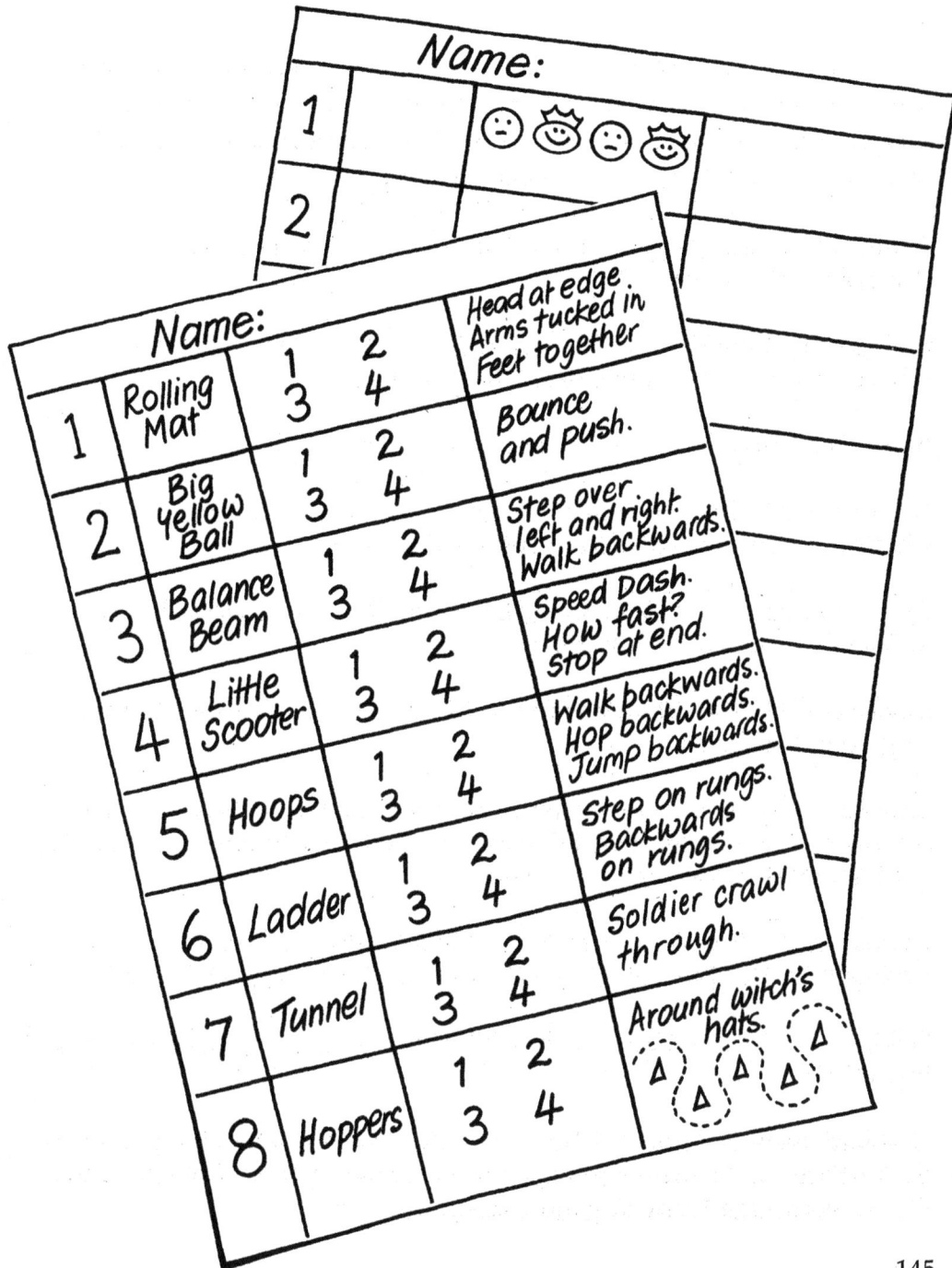

145

REFERENCES

ACHPER and the Australian Trampoline Sports Union Inc., *Trampoline Sports, Aussie Sports Coaching Program.* Endorsed by the Australian Coaching Council as an approved level O Coaching Course Manual. ACHPER Publications, 128 Glen Osmond Rd., Parkside, SA 5063. 1988.

Ayres, A.J., *Sensory Integration and Learning Disorders.* Western Psychological Services, 1973.

Braley, W.T., Konicki, G. and Leedy, C., *Daily Sensorimotor Activities.* Educational Activities, Freeport New York, 1985.

Buist, Dr.R., *Food Intolerance.* Harper and Collins, 1993

Delacato, C.H., *The Diagnosis and Treatment of Speech and Reading Problems.* Charles C. Thomas, Springfield, Illinois USA, 1963.

Delacato, C.H., *A New Start for the Child with Reading Problems*, David McKay Co. Ltd., New York, 1970.

Delacato, C.H., *The Ultimate Stranger*, Doubleday and Co. Inc., Garden City, New York, 1974.

Education Department of Western Australia, *The Fundamental movement skill assessment manual*, 1997, Education Department of Western Australia, 151 Royal Street, East Perth, WA 6004.

Getman, G.N., *How To Develop Your Child's Intelligence*, Research Publications, P.O. Box 636, White Plains, Md., USA, 20695-0636, 1962.

Gold, Svea J. *When Children Invite Child Abuse.* Eugene Oregan, Fernridge Press, 1986.

Goddard, Sally, *A Teacher's Window into the Child's Mind* and papers from the Institute for Neuro-physiological psychology. (INPP). Director Peter Blythe. Fernridge Press, Eugene Oregan USA 1996.

References

Happy, R.M., *Basketball Ball Handling*, Dribblers, 1995. Villa 8, 3 Isaac Place, Quakers Hill, NSW, 2763.

Hawke, M., *Nutrition and its Impact on Learning, Behaviour and Development*, ANSUA, Queensland, 1995.

Larkin, D. and Hoare, D., *Out of Step*. Department of Human Movement and Recreation Studies, University of Western Australia, Nedlands, W.A., 6009. 1991.

Pheloung, B., *Help Your Child To Learn, A practical guide for helping children with learning difficulties*. Bantam/Tortoiseshell Press, 1988.

Pheloung, B. and King, J., *Overcoming Learning Difficulties, How you can help a child who finds it hard to learn*. Doubleday, 1992.

Rigby J. and Hawke M., *The ANSUA Developmental School Program*, ANSUA Learning Centre, Queensland.

Rigby J., *Children with Specific Learning Difficulties: ANSUA'S Approach*, ANSUA Learning Centre, 1994.

Sasse, M., *If Only We'd Known..*,Toddler Kindy Gymbaroo P/L. 1979.

Tansley, A.E., *Reading and Remedial Reading*. Routledge and Kegan Paul, London, 1967.

ADDENDUM

STUDY OF SENSORY INTEGRATION COMBINED WITH REMEDIAL TEACHING METHODS
By Robin Taylor, Educational Clinical Psychologist
B.A. (Macq) M. A.(Syd) Dip. Clin Psych.(Syd)

I have been interested in learning problems for the past fifteen years. I became committed to assisting children and adults with learning difficulties after having had my two children Andrew and Matthew who both experience learning difficulties. I have witnessed the distress of children, their parents and adults with learning difficulties and the 'road blocks' to spelling, reading, arithmetic, writing and placing their thoughts onto paper. I found that combining movement to aid the remediation of learning difficulties was extremely successful.

I met Barbara Pheloung ten years ago, and she had experienced similar positive results and success using this approach with learning difficulties. I decided to prove what Barbara and I had experienced for many years. The results of this study indicate that spelling, reading, auditory short term memory, arithmetic and visual attention to detail made significant improvements using this approach.

The study in detail

It has been known for many years that movement has been of assistance in learning. Delacato (1963) has suggested that reading difficulties are the result of inadequate or incomplete neurological organisation.

If we are to understand learning difficulties, we must find the basic cause of the problem. The diagnosis must deal with the extent and type of neurological organisation, which has been achieved by the individual.

Movement and physical activity help the two sides of the brain work together and integrate. This needs to have occurred around the age of seven years so that the child can reach his full potential for academic tasks of various degrees of difficulty. Disordered sensory integration accounts for many aspects of learning disorders and enhancing sensory integration will make academic learning easier for those children whose problems are in that domain.

Sensory integration or the ability to organise sensory information can be improved through controlling its input to activate brain mechanisms. Piaget (1952), has stressed the importance of early sensory motor stimulation including the infant reflex stage. Each developmental stage assimilates part of the previous one. Piaget emphasises sensory integration and response to it as critical to the early origins of intelligence.

Ames and Ig (1964) emphasise the patterned, lawful and sequential manner of child's development. Larger underlying sensory integrative problems probably are related to previous developmental steps that had not matured properly. It is the child whose central nervous system has not developed in the normal manner which leaves him unable to organise a response and who becomes learning disabled.

Getman (1984) indicates that the foundation to every intellectual activity of the human being is the skill of directed movements and motor co-ordination. The efficiency of muscle use is a pre-requisite for the normal organisation of all knowledge of the world around us. All learning requires movement in some order. Unfortunately all movement does not guarantee learning and the most effective patterns need to be examined.

Some theorists who have experimented and found positive results are Getman, Ayres, Delacato, Tansley and Le Froy. The program described here was aimed at combining movement and learning and it attempts to measure the success of this approach.

Background of the experiment
Children with learning problems were identified by teaching staff and parents who filled in a checklist. The checklist was analysed by the remedial teacher and teachers to assess the appropriateness of this referral. If the referral was appropriate in Oxford Falls Grammar School the Wechsler Intelligence Scale, Key Maths, Schonell Spelling and Neale Analysis of Reading were administered.

In Illawarra Christian School the Wechsler Intelligence Scale, Schonell Spelling Test and Neale Analysis of Reading were administered. The children were retested on the above tests. The average time between testing of both groups was two years six months, after they had taken part in the program. The mean number of days that the two groups participated was 180 days, which spanned an average period of two and a half years. The control group emerged in both schools and consisted of children who were in need of remediation but did not participate in the program. The total number of children involved was 63; 42 participating in the program and 21 in the control group.

The summary given in Table 1 indicates which groups participated in the various tests. The programs written for each group of children (average 6.5 per group), were individually constructed for their specific problem areas.

Examples of the tasks in the programs and an example of an answer sheet filled in by those running each group are included. The volunteers, mostly parents, who ran each group were instructed in the method and marking procedures. Each program was changed for each individual group on an average of twelve weeks over an average period of two years six months.

Examples of the activities
a) Trampoline sequences.
b) Commando crawl.
c) Obstacle course using directionality, above, below etc.
d) Find a word on a blackboard using large arm movements.
e) Making words from plasticine.
f) Hammock - swinging.
g) Sequence of movements with auditory and visual instructions.
h) Visualising stories with movement.
i) Fine motor finger exercises.
j) Reproduction of abstract visual patterns with beads and blocks.
k) Visual and auditory memory games.
l) Jumping and counting on a number-line.
m) Angels in the snow - co-ordination exercises.
n) Crisscross exercises - motor co-ordination and organisational exercises.
o) Bean bag exercises with oral instructions.
p) Writing letters in a wet sand tray.
q) Writing words on backs of children.
r) Ball exercises with directionality.
s) Hopscotch and spelling exercises.

Examples of a typical answer sheet
(See Appendix 1V)

Analysis
A. Hypothesis testing – children with Sensory Integration improved significantly when compared with the control group.
Multivariate Repeated Measures Design
In this experiment, two measurements (before and after the Sensory Integration) are taken on the same student (experimental unit or subject)

TABLE ONE
Summary of tests performed in Oxford Falls and Illawarra Christian School

Tests	OF remedial group	IL remedial group	OF Control group	IL Control group
1. Reading Age	*	*	*	*
2. Spelling	*	*	*	*
3. Maths	*		*	
4. WISCIII	*	*		
5. Arithmetic	*	*		
6. Vocabulary	*	*		
7. Information	*	*		
8. Comprehension	*	*		
9. Digit Span	*	*		
10. Picture Completion	*	*		
11. Picture Arrangement	*	*		
12. Object Assembly	*	*		
13. Block Design	*	*		
14. Coding	*	*		
15. Mazes	*	*		

for each of the tests given. The tests common to both groups are reading and spelling. The measurements tend to correlate with each other within each test and across different tests. Thus a multivariate repeated measure analysis is used to account for this type of correlation. Two types of effects are examined, namely, the scores on each test before and after for each student (within-subject effect) and the effects between the Sensory Integration group and the control group (between-subject effect).

Four different data sets are used to test this hypothesis.
Data set A: Divide the students into two groups, the Sensory Integration group and control group. All the students are considered as coming from the same school. Only two between-subject effects are considered.
Data set B: Divide the students into four groups, the Sensory Integration groups and the control groups in two different schools. This is to account for the school effect in the analysis and thus four between-subject effects are present.
Data set C: Consider the Sensory Integration group and the control group in Oxford Falls only.
Data set D: Consider the Sensory Integration group and the control group in Illawarra Christian School only.

B. Analysis on the improvement made by the remedial group.
In order to investigate on what aspects the students improve most, the average percentage increases in scores for each test are computed and ranked. These computations are based on those students who have Sensory Integration learning only. The results are shown in Table 2.

Results

A. Hypothesis testing. Children with Sensory Integration improved significantly when compared with the control group.

For each data set, two hypotheses are examined by using the procedures GLM in the statistical software SAS. The tests are carried at 5 percent level of significance.

Hypothesis 1
There are no differences in improvement made between the two groups of children, that is, the Sensory Integration group and the control group make the same improvement. There are no differences for the performance before and after. The results are summarised in Table 3.

It is found that the Sensory Integration group and the control group performed differently when school effect is considered. Yet this difference is confounded when the school effect is ignored as the null hypothesis of no difference is accepted at p-value 0.2428. Therefore, performance on these two groups should be analysed individually.

B. Analysis on the improvement made by the Sensory Integration group.
The test results are based on the chronological age scores obtained by each student, thus it is biased to make comparisons on their increase in raw score only. As a result, the percentage increase in every test for each student is used instead. The average percentage increase is then calculated.

Students receiving Sensory Integration improved most significantly in digit span and arithmetic, the percentage increases are more than 38

TABLE TWO
Summary of hypothesis testing

Test	Data Set	null hypothesis 1	p-value	null hypothesis 2	p-value
Test 1	A	accept	0.2428	reject	0.0001
Test 2	B	reject	0.0001	reject	0.0001
Test 3	C	reject	0.0017	reject	0.0001
Test 4	D	reject	0.0187	reject	0.0001

TABLE THREE
Average percentage increase in each test and their respective ranking

Test	Oxford	rank	Illawarra	rank	all students*	rank
1. Reading Age	36.76%	4	34.75%	4	36.04.%	3
2. Spelling	34.67%	5	32%	6	33.72%	5
3. Maths	34.19%	6				
4. WISCIII	17.12%	13	14.94%	12	16.34%	12
5. Arithmetic	38.05%	2	39.56%	2	38.59%	2
6. Vocabulary	19.39%	12	12.24%	14	16.83%	11
7. Information	15.74%	14	13.74%	13	15.03%	13
8. Comprehension	14.26%	15	15.88%	11	14.84%	14
9. Digit Span	39.22%	1	42.62%	1	40.43%	1
10. Picture Completion	36.99%	3	32.66%	5	35.44%	4
11. Picture Arrangement	32.71%	7	31.67%	7	32.34%	6
12. Object Assembly	25.88%	8	28.02%	8	26.64%	8
13. Block Design	24.81%	9	35.28%	3	28.55%	7
14. Coding	24.05%	11	27.46%	9	25.27%	9
15. Mazes	24.34%	10	21.35%	10	23.27%	10

* average percentage increase of all the students who have received sensory integration in both

percent. However, their improvements on vocabulary, overall IQ, information and comprehension are not as high – the percentage increase for each is less than 20 percent. These results are shown in the histograms attached in the appendices.

Conclusions

It is found that the performance of the students on the tests before and after receiving Sensory Integration differ significantly when considering the students from individual schools. This difference is confounded once the school effect is ignored. The students improve most distinctively in digit span and arithmetic, and improved to a lesser extent in information, comprehension and vocabulary. Normally overall IQ would not improve if an intervention did not occur. Learning problems which are not remediated usually cause overall IQ scores to decrease over time.

However, the sample size of this experiment is not that effectively large, therefore the conclusions may not be extended in broad sense. Moreover, only two tests, spelling and reading, were completed by students in the control group. The average percentage increase for these two tests, spelling and reading, rank quite high among all the tests offered. This may favour the rejection of the hypothesis that there is no difference in the performance between these two groups. Groups receiving sensory integration have made positive gains.

Robyn Taylor B.A.(Macq) M.A.(Syd) DipClinPsych(Syd)
Educational / Clinical Psychologist

Appendix 1
Average percentage increase for students in Oxford Falls

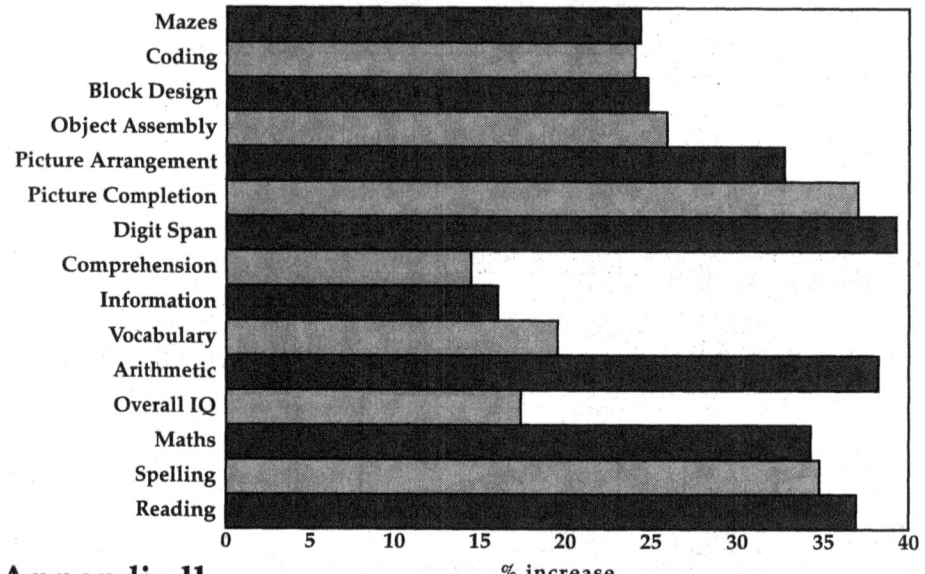

Appendix ll
Average percentage increase for students in Illawarra Christian School

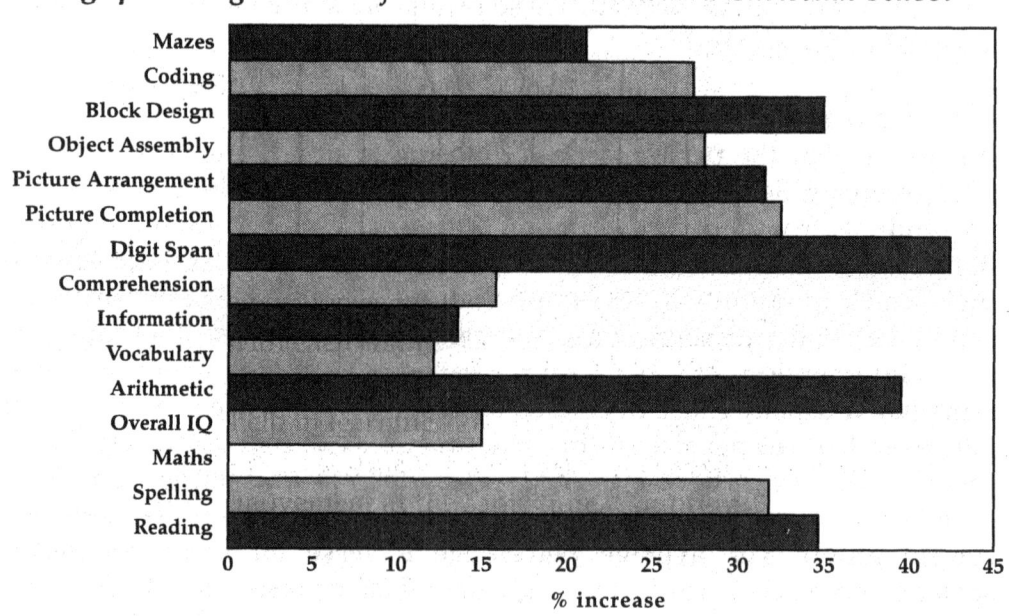

Appendix III
Average percentage increase for students having remedial learning

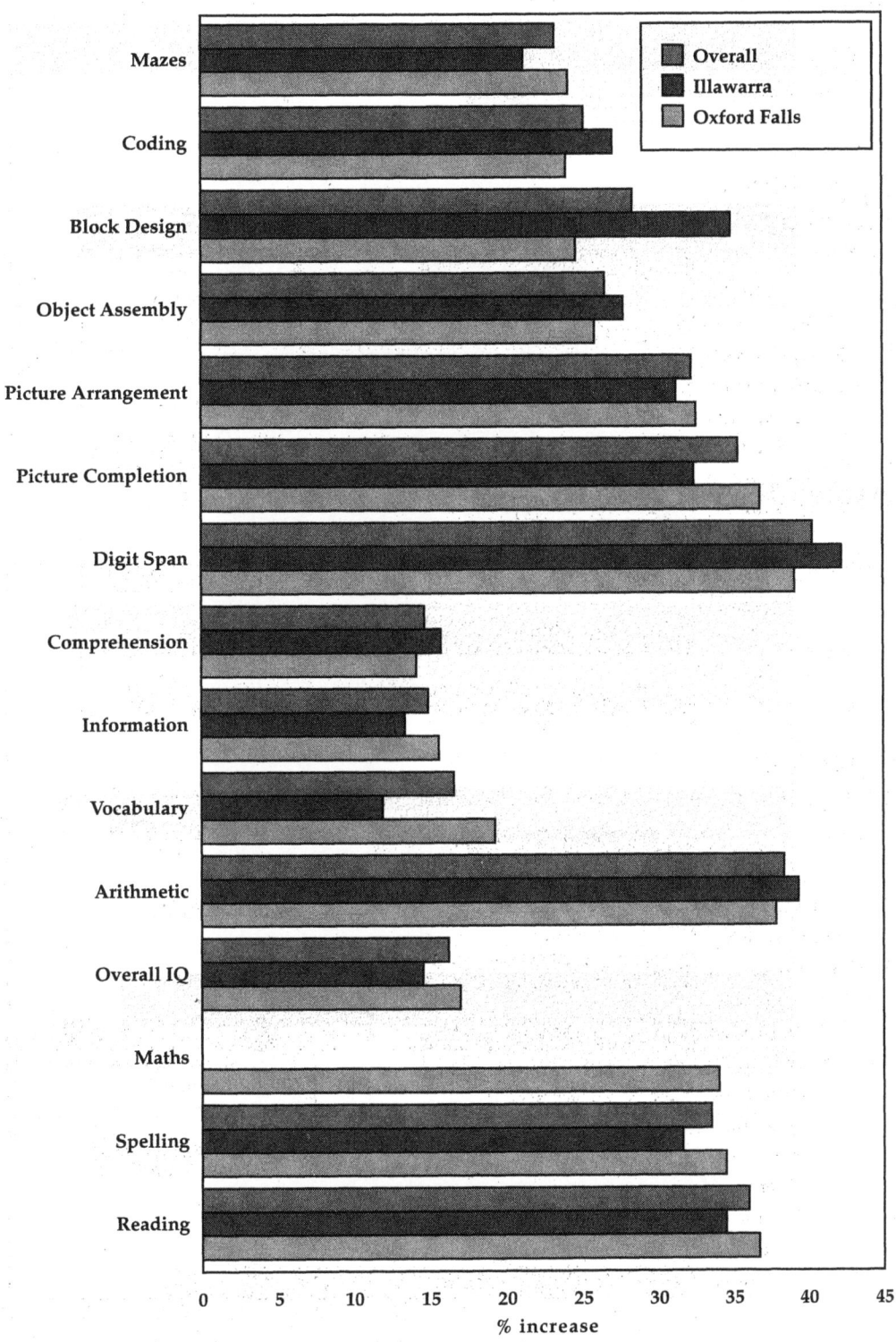

Appendix IV *Overall % increase in Illawarra Christian School*

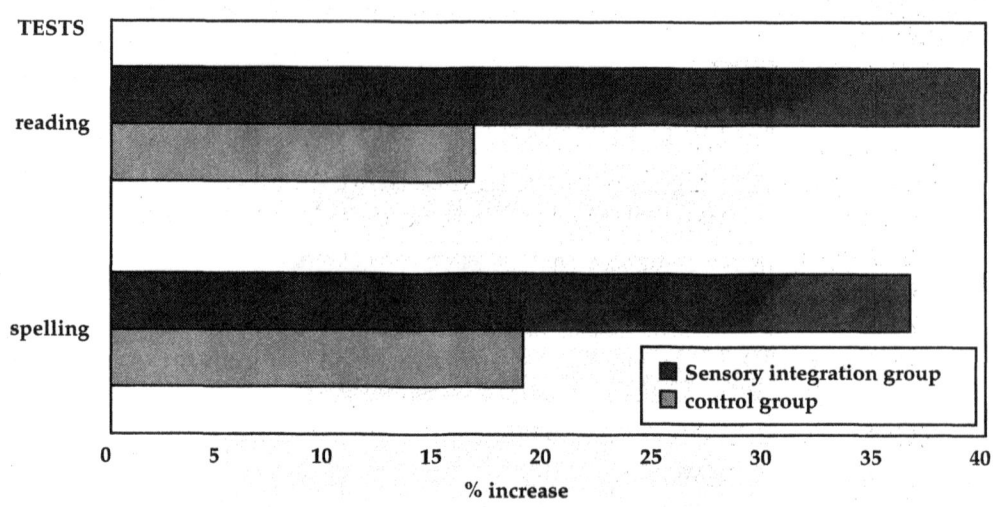

Appendix V *Overall % increase in Oxford Falls School*

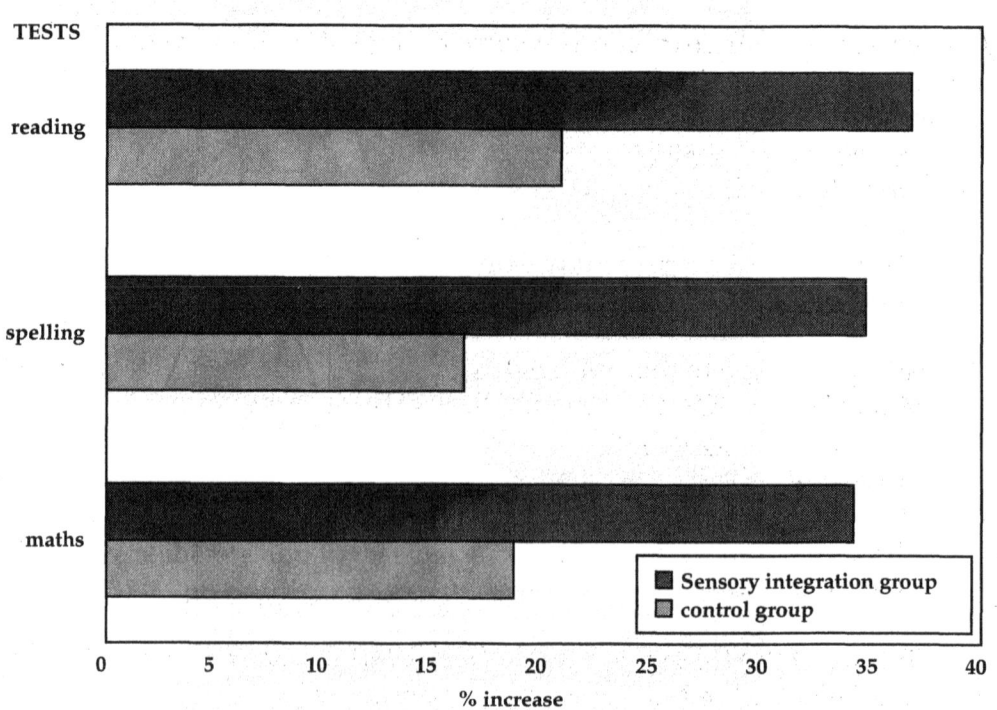

Addendum

Appendix VI *Scoring Sheets, Oxford Falls School*

EXAMPLE 1
GRADE 3   Name:_____Date:_____

1. Write list words for the class on back. Child has to guess the word (7 words each session). As this improves write a word incorrectly spelt from the list words, child has to say how it is incorrectly spelt.

   SCORE   COMMENTS: Write words here with a ✓or ✗ beside.
   Excellent ❏
   Good   ❏
   Poor   ❏
   Problem   ❏

2. ANGELS IN THE SNOW (co-ordination exercise)

   SCORE   COMMENTS:
   Excellent ❏
   Good   ❏
   Poor   ❏
   Problem   ❏

3. Give a set of oral instructions incorporating left, in front, behind, under, etc. Use plastic letters aim for 5-6 instructions. Ask the child to come back with the letters and make a word (4 a day).

   SCORE   COMMENTS:
   Excellent ❏
   Good   ❏
   Poor   ❏
   Problem   ❏

4. Read a paragraph to the child. Ask the question: 'What is the Main Idea?' SWIM IN HAMMOCK WHILST DOING THIS (2 Paragraphs)

   SCORE   COMMENTS:
   Excellent ❏
   Good   ❏
   Poor   ❏
   Problem   ❏

5. STILL IN THE HAMMOCK - LET THE CHILD READ A PARAGRAPH then ask 'What is the Main Idea in this paragraph.'

   SCORE   COMMENTS:
   Excellent ❏
   Good   ❏
   Poor   ❏
   Problem   ❏

| Help Your Class to Learn

6. Using a small pegboard give the child a written instruction (use directionality instructions – above, below, in front, right, left etc.)
Ask them to make 'A' five lines from the top and three lines from the left hand side. Then an 'S' – similar type of instruction, then a 'G'. Make a word – child must look at these letters and say what word they make.

    SCORE   COMMENTS:
    Excellent ❏
    Good   ❏
    Poor   ❏
    Problem ❏

7. TRAMPOLINE
    COMMENTS:

EXAMPLE 2
GRADE 2   Name:_____Date:_____
1. TRAMPOLINE
    COMMENTS:

2. SCOOTER BOARD
Left, right, under, over, etc (directionality).
Pick up letters.
Also add whole words which are scattered around i.e. CAT, POT.
Ask them to pick up words – select a few.
Use beam to walk along, use skipping rope, hammock.

Example:
I want you to go onto the scooter board and pick up the words cat, hand, sand and bring them back to me, then swing ten times in the hammock then pick up the ball with your right hand and bounce it on the right hand side of the hammock ten times. (This instruction will be too long for some so break it up until they can obtain that length.)

    SCORE   COMMENTS:
    Excellent ❏
    Good   ❏
    Poor   ❏
    Problem ❏

3. Give five words – one not in that word family. Child must say which one is not and why (five lots each day). These words are to be read to the child for them to 'listen' to not see e.g. Fat, Mat, Let, Cat (Let is different because it ends with et instead of at like the other words.)

SCORE COMMENTS:
Excellent ❑
Good ❑
Poor ❑
Problem ❑

4. Use Plasticine to make words (from spelling list). 'If time do seven' Write here words used and put a ✓ or ✗ beside to indicate right or wrong.

_____ ❑   _____ ❑
_____ ❑   _____ ❑
_____ ❑   _____ ❑
_____ ❑

5. HOPSCOTCH

13	14	15
10	11	12
7	8	9
4	5	6
1	2	3

Give sums like 2 + 5 =

They jump on 2 then 5 then the answer 7 (seven each session)

SCORE COMMENTS:
Excellent ❑
Good ❑
Poor ❑
Problem ❑

6. USE SAND TRAY - Write words in sand try - spelling words.

SCORE COMMENTS: Write words here with a ✓ or ✗ beside.
Excellent ❑
Good ❑
Poor ❑
Problem ❑

References
1. SAS/STAT *User's Guide Version 6*
   4th edition, Volume 2
2. *Multivariate analysis of variance and repeated measures*
   D.J.Hand & C.C.Taylor
3. *The Diagnosis And Treatment Of Speech And Reading Problems*
   C.H. Delacato
4. *Neurological Organisation and Reading*
   C.H.Delacato
5. *How to Develop your Child's Intelligence*
   G.N.Getman
6. *Reading and Remedial Reading*
   A.E.Tansley
7. *Towards Developmental Re-education*
   Peter Blythe
8. *Improving Literacy Through Motor Development*
   Rob Lefroy

Appendix
I   Histogram of the average percentage increase for students in Oxford Falls Grammar School.
II Histogram of the average percentage increase for students in Illawarra Christian School.
III Histogram of the average percentage increase for all students receiving remedial learning.
IV Overall percentage increase Illawarra Christian School.
V   Overall percentage increase Oxford Falls Grammar School.
VI Scoring sheets, Oxford Falls School.

Acknowledgments
I would like to thank my two sons, the parents, children and teachers from Illawarra Christian School and Oxford Falls Grammar School. Mr Geoff Hewitt, Principal at Illawarra Christian School, Mr Andrew Egan, Principal at Oxford Falls Grammar School, for their cooperation and never-ending support.

Thanks to my dear friends Barbara Pheloung and Dr Mary Lou Sheil who have encouraged and supported this research.

Thanks to Sue Middleton, Department of Statistics, University of New South Wales, and Marion Burford, Department of Marketing, University of New South Wales, for their assistance in computing and statistical analysis.

Thank you to all the adults/children and their parents who gave me the opportunity to acquire a greater understanding of learning difficulties.

www.ingramcontent.com/pod-product-compliance
Ingram Content Group UK Ltd.
Pitfield, Milton Keynes, MK11 3LW, UK
UKHW051652180426
11947UKWH00021B/1922